THE SYMBOL OF
THE FAITH

A *Study of*
THE APOSTLES' CREED

By GEORGE HEDLEY

THE MACMILLAN COMPANY · *New York*

1948

PRINTED IN THE UNITED STATES OF AMERICA
BY THE VAIL-BALLOU PRESS, INC., BINGHAMTON, N. Y.

I BELIEVE in God the Father Almighty, Maker of heaven and earth:

And in Jesus Christ his only Son our Lord: Who was conceived by the Holy Ghost, Born of the Virgin Mary: Suffered under Pontius Pilate, Was crucified, dead, and buried: He descended into hell; The third day he rose again from the dead: He ascended into heaven, And sitteth on the right hand of God the Father Almighty: From thence he shall come to judge the quick and the dead.

I believe in the Holy Ghost: The holy Catholic Church; The Communion of Saints: The Forgiveness of sins: The Resurrection of the body:

And the Life everlasting.

Amen.

FOREWORD

Once again the questions raised by students at Mills College have forced an attempt to bring together old history and current meaning. Fourteen of the seventeen chapters which follow, took form originally as sermons in the College Chapel, in the spring of 1947. The first announcement of the series described it as 'an effort to interpret the Apostles' Creed in terms both of its history and of modern ways of thinking. It is to be hoped that it will be of service alike to those who have accepted the Creed without much pondering of its content, and to those who have rejected its content because they think it incompatible with current thought and knowledge.'

Parts of a few of the sermons, in their original form, appeared in the Mills College *Weekly*, whose editor has graciously accorded me permission to reprint those sections. In the present text I have eliminated a number of purely local and temporary references, such as one to the campus sins of academic indifference and of social over-exertion; but I have retained elements of conversational tone, including occasional use of the first person singular. The wholly new chapters are 6, 8, and 17, dealing respectively with the silence of the Creed about Jesus' teaching ministry, with the 'descent into hell,' and with the relationship of faith to understanding.

It should be emphasized that this little book is not, and does not pretend to be, a compendium of Christian theology. It is a brief and simple discussion of some questions raised in the modern mind by the phrasing of an ancient Creed; and an attempt to identify the living values which from the first that phrasing sought to convey.

In general I have made much more use of ancient than of modern authors, on the ground that those who were engaged in writing the Creed are the best qualified to tell us of its meaning. Quotations from the Fathers appear in my own renderings from the original texts. For those who care to check references, and to follow further some minor details of argument, a body of notes is appended to the text. Wherever possible I have cited patristic references as they appear in the Migne series, and classical materials according to the editions of the Loeb Classical Library.

The reader is entitled to a summary indication of basic point of view. Obviously any writer considers his own views 'orthodox,' in the sense that for him they represent 'right teaching.' More specifically, however, the 'orthodoxy' of these chapters seeks to avoid both of the current major heresies of American Protestantism: the 'modernist' and the 'fundamentalist.' With reference to Jesus the Christ, who is crucial in the Christian Creed, it shares neither the Apollinarian denial of the human Jesus, nor the Unitarian rejection of the eternal Christ.

This will not keep heretics on either side of these fences from assigning the author to the opposite school of false teachers. He readily confesses his indebtedness to both of them. No school of teaching which has survived for any length of time may be discarded as being wholly false; and both Apollinarianism and Socinianism remain with us. In general, I would suggest that the heretics commonly are right in what they affirm, but that both groups are usually wrong when they attempt to deny.

My own affirmations I dedicate, in humble gratitude, to the memory of George Croft Cell; who, more than a quarter-century ago, in the School of Theology at Boston University, drove me to study the history of the Creed; and thereby led me toward the discovery of a *Credo* which I may call my own.

G. H.

Mills College
St. Stephen's Day
1947

LIST OF ABBREVIATIONS

ARG . . . Translation by Alex. R. Gordon in *The Complete Bible: An American Translation* (Chicago, 1939).

ARV . . . American Standard Edition of the Revised Version, 1901.

AV . . . 'Authorised' ('King James') Version, 1611.

EJG . . . Translation by Edgar J. Goodspeed in *The Complete Bible* (see ARG, above).

ERV . . . (English) Revised Version, 1885.

GH . . . The author.

JM . . . Translation by James Moffatt in *The Holy Bible: A New Translation* (New York, 1924).

LCL . . . Loeb Classical Library.

PG . . . J. P. Migne, *Patrologiae Cursus Completus,* Greek series (Paris, 1857 and after).

PL . . . The same, Latin series (Paris, 1844 and after).

RSV . . . Revised Standard Version of the New Testament, 1946.

CONTENTS

1. *I BELIEVE: I DO NOT SEE*

'I believe . . . '—The Apostles' Creed.
'Faith is assurance of things hoped for, a conviction of things not seen.'—Hebrews 11:1 (ARV).
'Blessed are they that have not seen, and yet have believed.'—St. John 20:29 (AV).

When I was a great deal younger than I am now, and literal in mind, as youth so often is, I found myself in trouble about reciting the Apostles' Creed in the services of the Church. In its text were some statements that I had come to think untrue in fact; and in respect for my own intellectual integrity, as I conceived it, I decided I could not join in saying those things. Accordingly I kept my mouth tightly shut while the rest of the congregation recited 'born of the Virgin Mary' and 'the resurrection of the body.'

Soon it dawned upon me that in order to be consistent I would have to be silent also for 'conceived by the Holy Ghost,' and for all the latter series of declarations about Jesus Christ: 'He descended into hell; The third day he rose again from the dead: He ascended into heaven, And sitteth on the right hand of God the Father Almighty: From thence he shall come to judge the quick and the dead.'

Leaving out all these clauses left me, of course, very nearly speechless. Soon philosophical questions about the nature and activity of God forbade my saying the opening clause; and then doubts of the trustworthiness of the Gospel records stopped me from narrating the events of Jesus' earthly life. I found myself left, finally, with nothing but 'the holy Catholic Church'; and since I had some quite reasonable doubts both about the Church's historic holiness and about its real universality, I was reduced at last to whispering the two adjectives, and coming out strongly only on the single noun 'Church.'

1

All this time, however, I still was standing up when the congregation stood to say the Creed; and I was standing in the Church. Thus in two ways for me the Church had managed to survive my own aggressive scepticism. The Church did remain in the Creed, and the Creed remained in the Church. That puzzled me: puzzled me enough to challenge me to enquire further.

Ultimately I began to move toward an answer which has proved more and more nearly sufficient for me. I am no more able today, than I used to be, to assert the factuality of the credal statements. Some of them, indeed, now seem to me even less tenable, in literal terms, than they did at the outset. Nevertheless I can and do today recite the Creed in a clear voice and in a clear conscience; and also, I believe, with an honest mind. I can do this because I have learned something of how the Creed came into being, something of what it meant when first it was put together, and of what it has meant throughout the centuries of Christian history. The answer, I learned, did indeed lie in the Church: in the history of the Church, and in the history of the Creed within the Church.

This book is an attempt to retrace the path of enquiry which I followed. Since the path led through Church History, it is through Church History that we must follow it. To some this may seem a fearsome prospect. It nevertheless is one we must face, if we are to know what the Creed is about. The reason for facing it is that knowing what the Creed really is about will help us to know what life itself is about.

We are attempting the study of a very ancient verbal formula. It is old, but it was the product of genuine life. It is old, but once it was wholly contemporary, highly modern. It is old, but it has stayed alive until now; and its evident survival value is enough to require its serious consideration from the standpoint of today.

The Apostles' Creed is not quite so old as its name might suggest. An engaging but late legend has it that, when the disciples were gathered together on the day of Pentecost, they spontaneously compiled the Creed from individual and unplanned contributions.[1] 'I believe,' said St. Peter, 'in God the Father Almighty, maker of heaven and earth.' 'And in Jesus Christ, his only Son our Lord,' added St. Andrew. 'Who was conceived by the Holy Ghost, born of Mary the Virgin,' supplemented St. James. And so on. . . .

The less romantic fact is that the 'Apostles' Creed,' in substantially the form in which we know it, seems to have taken definite shape in the western Churches during the fourth century A.D.: that is, just after Constantine's acceptance of Christianity, and just before the capture of the city by the barbarians of the North. A revised version of the text, in all essentials the same as that which now we use, appears in a sermon attributed to Caesarius of Arles, delivered during the sixth century.[2] (The succeeding chapter of this present study, discussing 'The Apostles' Creed in the Churches,' will review the early history of the Creed in greater detail.)

Church historians refer to the fourth-century document as 'The Old Roman Symbol.' That name is worth noting, for it suggests the real nature and use of the Apostles' Creed in the developing Christian community. It indicates what indeed was the fact, that to accept the Apostles' Creed was to wear the badge of accepted Christian membership. The other great creeds of Christendom: that of Nicea, its revision at Constantinople, the formula of Chalcedon: [3] all of them much longer and much more elaborate than this one, were written and voted upon in successive formal Councils of the worldwide Church. This one which we call 'the Apostles' Creed,' however, took its shape gradually, informally, almost anonymously. It grew into the usage of the Church, because it had grown in the consciousness of the Church's people. It has been modified in detail from time to time, and by all sorts of individuals and communities.

What exactly is meant by calling the Creed a 'Symbol'? Light is thrown upon that question by a name for it which was current still earlier. The incipient formula of the second century, which begins to appear in the writings of the early Western Church Fathers, was by them called the *regula fidei*, the 'rule of faith.' Now a rule (or, as we would say, a ruler) has two functions. It is used indeed for the drawing of lines, and in that way it controls action. Much more importantly, a rule is an instrument for measuring. Since no one of the several forms of the Apostles' Creed ever was authoritatively set forth by the whole of the ancient Church, the 'rule of faith' must be thought of chiefly as a generally accepted basis of measurement, rather than as an absolute and specific means of control. The Creed did not tell people what they should believe. Rather it classified people on the basis of what they did believe.

What was a Christian? Who were to be recognised as Christians? Religious thinking and practice in the Greco-Roman world were chaotic; and thinking and practice even within the comparatively small Christian group quickly had become multiform and no little confused. When at last Christianity was officially tolerated by the government, and soon after that was officially established as the state religion, clear identifications and precise distinctions seemed more important than they had been before. Questions of individual status and of Church property necessarily were involved; and still more significantly, questions of personal genuineness which had not arisen while being a Christian was unpopular and even dangerous. Now that the Church drew all comers, it faced the risk of losing its own true character in the muddle of its new, greatly enlarged, and highly miscellaneous membership.

Some degree of difference was tolerable, and was tolerated. Other departures from the tradition seemed to strike at the very heart of the organic life of Christianity. Among these were numerous survivals of the ideas and characters of the old pagan gods; the sharp separation that late Greek thought had asserted as between matter and spirit; a consequent denial that Jesus could have lived a genuine human life; and above all the disposition of a few arrogantly to claim for themselves special knowledge which was outside the reach of the common man.

At all of these points of doubt and dispute the Apostles' Creed was decisively clear. It stated categorically the truly human origin and experience of Jesus. (The reference to Jesus' being 'born of the Virgin Mary,' for example, was a declaration not so much that God was his father as that a human woman was his mother; and it was the direct answer to a large school of heretics who were declaring that Jesus had no human nature at all.) The Creed also rejected any notion of fundamental opposition between the spiritual and the material realms of life. Centrally it stated the essentials of the Christian faith, of the primary Christian tradition as distinguished from later heresies, in terms that any layman could understand.

The details of the accepted points of view, and of the approved emphases, it will be our business to consider in the chapters that follow; and the details then should come clearer than they can be made in one summary paragraph. The essential fact for us to note here is that the Creed was the *regula fidei:* the 'rule of faith' as the yardstick of Christian loyalty. He who stayed close to it, he who embarked on no wide deviation from it, was recognized as belonging to the fellowship. This 'rule of faith' thus became also 'the old Roman Symbol': the simple symbol of true Christian oneness in the complex Roman world.

It is at this point, I think, that we must enter upon our own enquiry into the Creed's nature and meaning. It is from this point of view that we must see the Creed as a factor in our own thinking and life. I have said that the Church seemed to me still real and important, even in those youthful days when almost all of the Church's theology was eluding my grasp. From this one position maintained, I found myself able gradually to move back over the rest of the terrain: but in a new way and at a different level, in a way and at a level that more nearly satisfied my mind and heart. It was the Church which in my moral realization had survived the onslaught of my literal way of thinking. It was the Church, I came to see, that had created the Creed in the first place; and it was the Church alone that could make and keep the Creed alive.

But the Church, being a company of human beings, necessarily was limited both in its intellectual grasp and in its verbal skill. The Church could think and speak no better than could its members. What it could think was what the members were capable of thinking. What it could say was what they had the words to say. Thinking was and is conditioned by cultural background, speech by the subtle but sometimes stubborn factor of a given language. What at any time these people thought, therefore, was not necessarily final for them, let alone for us; and what they thought is but imperfectly revealed to us in the words they used. What mattered was what they tried to think, what on the basis of their thinking they tried to say. In short, the Creed is not the faith in itself. It is the Symbol of a faith toward which the Christians together were searching.

Once I had reached this stage of understanding, I found myself set free to utter the words of the Creed, all of the words, without any feeling of intellectual dishonesty or of moral guilt. Not the words, nor the apparent, immediate, limited sense of the words, really constituted the Creed. The Creed was rather a token of continuing fellowship in a human quest toward things divine; and my own reciting of it was thus my declaration of my own intent to share in that fellowship and in that quest. The Creed is something other, and greater, than a statement of details of opinion. It is a living bond of unity among Christians of every kindred, of every speech, of every age in history.

What the words themselves meant to the first phrase-makers we may guess, we may deduce, but we cannot certainly know; and probably the words never meant quite the same to any two persons who used them. What the words may mean to us we shall proceed to enquire; though almost certainly not many readers will agree as to all details of their meaning. What ultimately the Creed signifies is not words, but spirit: a spirit of unity, a spirit of loyalty, a spirit of sharing in a common search.

It is, let it be said again, a search and not a settlement. And so we come at last to the title of this opening chapter: 'I Believe: I Do Not See.' 'Blessed are they,' declares the fourth Gospel, 'who have not seen, and yet have believed.' 'Faith,' defines the unknown author of the letter to the Hebrews, 'is . . . a conviction of things not seen.' Believing is not seeing; and faith is not demonstrable fact. That distinction is basic to our whole enquiry. 'It is not possible,' argued St. Thomas Aquinas, 'that the same thing may be both seen and believed by the same person.' [4] The great modern Catholic theologian Etienne Gilson describes a true follower of Aquinas as 'a man who does not like to believe what he can know, and who never pretends to know what can be but believed.' [5]

That is to say, the realms of knowledge and of faith are separate and distinct, and must not be confused one with the other. The Creed of necessity is in the realm of faith, not in that of information. They who put together the words of the 'rule of faith' did not know that these things which they said were true. Neither do we know: nor can we ever. Not knowing these things true, yet they who declared them held them to be true: which was a different, a more difficult, and a more important, achievement of man's intellect and heart. They could hold them true because in their world they were intellectually conceivable. Much more vitally, they did hold them true because for them they were morally real.

Let us recognize and declare now that much which was intellectually conceivable in the first Christian century, or in the fourth, is not so in the twentieth: is not so for us, who inherit the Christian tradition and the Creed as a part of it. Literary and historical criticism, scientific method, philosophical judgment, have denied the literal veracity of some items which in the Creed are stated as if they were matters of external fact. These pages will not be devoted either to defending, or to explaining away, those details which to a reasonable modern mind show themselves to be factually in error. The moral value is something else again: and something much greater. What these men and women declared about God, about Jesus, about the Holy Ghost, represented for them something other than, and something more than, historical detail and theological framework. It represented what made their life worth living; and that kind of worthfulness may be just as available to us as it was to them.

If we were writing the Creed from an absolutely fresh start in our own time, we no doubt would phrase it quite differently. We are not so writing it, and I for one am not eager that we should. None of the numerous newly written creeds of our day, patly logical as most of them are, and elaborately guarded so as not to conflict with the most recently published hypotheses of science: none of these new creeds have gained any general acceptance or use. The role of the Creed as the rule of faith, as the Symbol of fellowship, hinges upon its historic character. It depends upon its very age, upon that unity throughout the centuries which its united repetition signifies.

Believing is not seeing. We shall not accept the old formula in its literal detail merely because it is old. Neither shall we be so naïve as to think that we can construct a new series of a hundred words which will be logically watertight for us and for all our successors. If first we do believe in the holy universal Church as the continuing fellowship of the faithful, we as members of that fellowship rightly and reasonably may enquire, may reëstimate, may reinterpret, as our own training and experience allow and suggest. This, after all, is just what the Church did from the beginning, and has done through all the years.

It must be admitted, and it should be asserted, that at least a minimum act of faith is requisite even to the starting of an enquiry such as this. At least we must believe that these early Christians were not dishonest, and that they were not fools. At least we must believe that a form of words which has lived so long could have done so only because it conveyed some values that were and are alive.

Starting with this minimum of faith, we may proceed to test the values by the evidence of life. The old words are not fully adequate, and no words ever will be. Our conviction of things unseen must be examined, evaluated, measured, over and over again, and by every instrument and every criterion that we can discover or devise. It is good that the Creed presents difficulties to us. Did it not, we would be the less challenged to think and to grow, and thus the less able to add our own gifts to the living tradition of Christendom. It is good also that the Creed offers meanings which have stood the test of time. Did it not, we would lack soil and nourishment for our own growing.

We do not see the unseen. We shall not, before the end of life. We still may be assured in our hope, convinced in our estimate of values. Not seeing fully, yet we may believe vitally. Our faith is deeper than mere opinion, and more alive. This is what we mean when we say 'I believe.'

2. THE APOSTLES' CREED IN THE CHURCHES

*'Baptizing them into the name of the Father and of the Son
and of the Holy Ghost.'*—St. Matthew 28:19 (ERV).
*'The rule of faith, indeed, is wholly one, alone immovable
and unchangeable.'*—Tertullian, about A.D. 205 [1]

The text from the Gospel according to St. Matthew ought perhaps to be cited rather from the *Didache,* 'The Teaching of the Twelve Apostles,' [2] which was a sort of handbook for the conduct of Church life, widely circulated in the middle of the second century A.D. Certainly it is clear that the triple, or Trinitarian, formula of baptism was not familiar to most of the New Testament writers, who speak of baptism simply 'into the name of Jesus.' [3] On the whole it seems more probable that the Trinitarian phrasing was reflected back into the Gospel text from the *Didache,* or from a similar source, than that the Gospel phrasing served as origin of the later usage.[4]

In any event, the connection of the triple formula with the rite of baptism is the essential clue to the Creed's first function in the Church. The baptizing of adults was the symbol of their personal acceptance of Christianity. What therefore was needed in the baptismal ceremony was a brief summary of the Christian position, simple enough to be understood by the laity, decisive as to distinctions from paganism and from current heresies, positive in identifying the position of the recognized Christian believer. As will be noted later, it was precisely in the ritual for baptism that the Creed served its principal purpose in the usage of the Church of the middle ages and after.

It will readily be seen that our present Creed is structurally an expansion of the triple baptismal formula, made by the inclusion of further detail about the Father and the Son, and by the appending of references to the Church, the forgiveness of sins, and the life to come. This process of expansion went on, and can be

10

traced, from the beginning of the second century until the Creed took its definitive form some four or five hundred years later. There is by no means room here to cite all the documentary evidence; but a few samples will serve to illustrate the course of development.

St. Ignatius, the Bishop of Smyrna who suffered martyrdom in A.D. 117, several times presents what seems to be a germinal creed. The clearest example appears in his letter to the Trallians:

Do not listen, therefore, when anyone speaks to you apart from Jesus Christ, who truly was born from the seed of David, and from Mary; who ate and drank; who truly suffered under Pontius Pilate, truly was crucified, and died. . . . He also truly was raised from the dead, his Father raising him, in the same way as his Father also will raise us who believe in him in Christ Jesus, without whom we have not the true life.[5]

Similarly St. Justin the Martyr, at about the middle of the century, writes in what seems to be a rapidly crystallizing formula. Thus, in his *First Apology*, he declares:

Our teacher of these things, born to this end, is Jesus Christ, who was crucified under Pontius Pilate. . . . We shall show that we worship him with reason, having learned him to be the Son of the living God, and holding him in the second place, and the prophetic Spirit in the third.[6]

St. Irenaeus of Lyons, who flourished about A.D. 180, has by some scholars been credited with carrying the incipient Creed from his native Asia Minor (or Syria) into Gaul. While he nowhere sets forth a credal text very close to the now accepted form, he provides within his famous treatise *Against Heresies*, as Professor A. C. McGiffert pointed out a generation ago,[7] most of the basic materials from which a full text of the Creed might be assembled. Of the numerous significant passages we may note especially this one:

The Church . . . has received from the apostles and from their disciples this faith, which is in one God, the Father almighty, who made heaven and earth, and the sea, and all things that are in them;

and in one Christ Jesus the Son of God, who became flesh for our salvation; and in the Holy Ghost . . . and the birth from a Virgin, and the suffering, and the rising from among the dead, and the bodily ascension into the heavens, of the beloved Christ Jesus our Lord, and his coming from the heavens in the glory of the Father.[8]

It will occur to many readers that this paragraph from St. Irenaeus contains seeds not only of the Apostles' Creed, but also of the formula adopted in A.D. 325 at the Council of Nicea. The insistence on the *one* God, and on *one* Christ Jesus, is a direct reply to the 'Gnostic' heresies which sought to separate the divine beings into multiple manifestations. As time went on this dispute faded into the background. Accordingly the stress upon the divine unity seemed now less essential, and specific reference to the singleness of God and of the Christ dropped out of the flexible phrasing of the Apostles' Creed while it remained in the fixed formula of Nicea.

Emphasis upon the absolute fixity of the 'rule of faith' comes first and most clearly from the North African lawyer Tertullian: who, alas! himself fell ultimately under condemnation as a heretic. The 'immovable and unchangeable' rule, as he stated it a year or two before he left the fellowship of the Church, is the following:

Believing, to wit, in one God Almighty, creator of the world, and in his Son Jesus Christ, born of the Virgin Mary, crucified under Pontius Pilate, the third day raised from the dead, received into heaven, seated now at the right hand of the Father, to come to judge living and dead through the resurrection of the flesh.[9]

In numerous other passages Tertullian offers brief summaries of the cardinal teaching of the Church of his time. While these are essentially the same in content, and include some identities of phrasing, they are by no means assimilated to a single formula.[10] We must conclude therefore that when Tertullian speaks of the 'rule of faith' as being 'immovable and unchangeable,' he is thinking of the essential content of that rule, and not specifically of a determined and authorized code of words.

Though the authoritative statement of orthodox doctrine was adopted by the Council at Nicea in the year 325, that formula evidently failed to displace in common usage, at least in the West, the briefer, less official statement whose growth we have been tracing. In A.D. 337 we find one Marcellus, Bishop of Ancyra in central Asia Minor, writing to Pope Julius I in an effort to establish his own orthodoxy. Though Marcellus is known as a leading defender of the Nicene position, he summarizes his own views in what evidently he considers the standard formula that will be recognized by the Church in Rome. This statement, addressed to the Roman Bishop from far away in the East, stands as the first decisive example of the 'old Roman Symbol' as the direct ancestor of our own Apostles' Creed. Translated from the Greek of Marcellus, the text reads:

I believe in God Almighty; and in Christ Jesus, his only Son our Lord, born of the Holy Ghost and Mary the Virgin, under Pontius Pilate crucified and buried, and the third day raised from the dead, ascended into heaven, and seated on the right hand of the Father, whence he shall come to judge living and dead; and in the Holy Ghost, the holy Church, the forgiveness of sins, the resurrection of the flesh.[11]

Two generations later, about A.D. 400, a western Christian wrote an 'Exposition of the Symbol.' It is evident that Rufinus of Aquileia regarded the Creed as being already of high antiquity and firm establishment. Nevertheless his version clearly is dependent on a Greek original, probably very similar to, if not identical with, that supplied in the letter of Marcellus.[12] The single change that Rufinus seems to make, aside from some clumsy ablatives which the later Latin versions of the Creed avoided, is the use of two different prepositions, *de* and *ex,* in the phrase relating to the birth 'of the Holy Ghost and (from) Mary the Virgin.' Since the change of *ex,* 'from,' to *et,* 'and,' would make Rufinus' entire clause an exact translation of Marcellus' Greek, it is tempting to suppose that *ex* is a variation introduced by later copyists rather than by Rufinus himself.

What is known as the 'received text' of our Creed took its
final form during the years that followed. In substance, as was
noted above, it is already complete in a sermon by Caesarius of
Arles, about a century after Rufinus. The process of accretion
can be recognized if we set together the text of Rufinus and the
version generally accepted in the West by the end of the eighth
century.[18]

Rufinus	*'Received' text*
I believe in God the Father Almighty;	I believe in God the Father Almighty, maker of heaven and earth;
and in Christ Jesus his only Son our Lord;	and in Jesus Christ his only Son our Lord;
who was born of the Holy Ghost from Mary the Virgin,	who was conceived of the Holy Ghost, born from Mary the Virgin,
who was crucified under Pontius Pilate, and buried;	suffered under Pontius Pilate, was crucified, dead, and buried;
(he descended into hell); [14]	he descended into hell;
the third day rose from among the dead,	the third day rose from among the dead,
ascended into the heavens,	ascended into the heavens,
sits at the right hand of the Father,	sits at the right hand of God the Father Almighty,
whence he shall come to judge living and dead;	whence he shall come to judge living and dead.
and in the Holy Ghost,	I believe in the Holy Ghost,
the holy Church,	the holy Catholic Church, the communion of saints,
the forgiveness of sins,	the forgiveness of sins,
the resurrection of the flesh.	the resurrection of the flesh, the life everlasting.

It appears from this comparison that the changes made after the time of Rufinus were principally by way of expansion, and stated what seemed to be natural implications of the phrasing as first it had been worked out. 'Maker of heaven and earth' elaborates rather than alters the expression of faith in God, even as did the insertion of 'the Father' at an earlier date. 'Suffered' and 'dead' might be thought to stress the reality of the passion as against Gnostic docetism, the denial of that reality; but since the controversy now was long past, it is more probable that these seemed to later Christians to be simply an obvious completion of the record. Possible doctrinal and apologetic aspects of the additions 'conceived of (the Holy Ghost),' 'he descended into hell,' 'the communion of saints,' and 'the life everlasting,' may best be considered when we come to detailed consideration of these phrases in subsequent chapters.

For liturgical purposes the Creed of Nicea, carrying the formal authority of the Church expressed in its first great Council, secured and retained the chief position. In slightly varying forms it still is central in the liturgies of all the Eastern Churches, in the Roman Mass, and in the Communion service of the Anglican groups. It was in the baptismal ritual rather than in the Eucharist that the Apostles' Creed, as a simpler formula setting forth the essential faith of the individual Christian, served its major function. With the development of infant baptism as the general practice of the Church, this function of the Creed became less prominent, though its phrasing still was used as a part of the charge to the godparents. (In the Eastern Churches the Nicene Creed is used in the baptismal service, as it is in the Eucharist. In these Churches, of course, the Apostles' Creed never has had even semi-official standing.)

By about the eighth or ninth century, the Apostles' Creed came into daily use in two of the 'Lesser Hours' of Western monastic devotions: the services of Prime, early in the morning, and of Compline, late in the evening. Here it is evident that the

Creed was regarded less as a test of orthodoxy than as an expression of Christian loyalty, and as a basis for Christian meditation. The use of the Creed in the Anglican services of Morning and Evening Prayer derives directly from its occurrence in these devotional exercises, as Prime was combined with Mattins and Compline with Vespers.

With the Protestant Reformation, and the attendant translation of the services into national languages, the Creed underwent further though minor modifications. In the German text of the Lutheran service (which is either the full Eucharist or the ante-Communion) 'the holy Catholic Church' becomes *die heilige christliche Kirche*, 'the holy Christian Church.' This presumably reflects the intensity of Lutheran reaction against 'Catholic' claims. Nevertheless in the Latin text which remained official in Lutheranism the reading *sanctam ecclesiam catholicam* was retained.

The English translation, presumably made by Archbishop Cranmer, contains only one notable variant from the clear meaning of the Latin and the Greek. This is the reading 'resurrection of the body,' where the Greek has *sarkos anastasin* and the Latin *carnis resurrectionem,* both of them unmistakably 'resurrection of the flesh.' While this modification no doubt has served to ease the intellectual problem of some modern Christians, by seeming to permit the sort of distinction which St. Paul made between the 'natural body' and the 'spiritual body,' it is unlikely that the English reformers thought in these terms. That the change rather was casual and almost accidental is suggested by the fact that in the interrogative form in the baptismal service, and in the order for the visitation of the sick, the English Prayer Book preserved the reading, 'the resurrection of the flesh.' The Prayer Books of the American Episcopal Church, from the first of them in 1789, have provided in the baptismal service simply for reference to the Creed rather than for its recitation, and so at this point have eliminated the contrast in rendering. 'The resurrection of the flesh' remained in the American order for the visitation of the sick until the Prayer Book of 1929, when the Creed was omitted from this service.

The clause 'he descended into hell' has occasioned special difficulty in modern thinking. It is striking that this also seems to have troubled the American ecclesiastics in the earliest days of this nation. The Prayer Book of 1789 provided that the statement either might be omitted altogether, or might be said in the form, 'He went into the place of departed spirits.' The question as to whether the choice rested in the hands of the local parish or in those of the diocese never was settled officially, in view of the fact that the option seems never to have been exercised by either. In 1892 the permission to omit was dropped from the Prayer Book, though the substitute still is indicated as permissible.

While John Wesley retained in his Sunday Service (prepared for the American Methodist societies in 1784) the full text of the Creed as it was used in England, including this clause, the Methodist Episcopal Church eliminated the reference to hell. The Lutheran Churches in America have retained it, apparently without the occurrence of any serious discussion. Perhaps the most curious history connected with this phrase, in recent times, is that of its treatment in the *Book of Common Worship* of the Presbyterian Church in the United States of America (Northern). It seems that the actual compilation of the successive editions of this book is made by a Committee of the General Assembly, which latter body commonly has given its approval *en bloc*. In the edition of 1906 the 'hell' clause carried a footnote reading, '*i.e.*, he continued in the state of the dead, and under the power of death, until the third day.' In 1932 the footnote was shortened to read, 'He continued in the state of the dead until the third day.' In the most recent revision, that of 1946, the comment has been dropped altogether.

There continues to be much of flexibility in the use of the Creed's words and phrases. Despite the official formula of Presbyterianism, as represented in its service book, a number of local Presbyterian Churches have seen fit to omit 'He descended into hell.' Since 1935 the American Methodist ritual has read 'Holy Spirit' instead of 'Holy Ghost.' In Methodist practice the word 'again' is omitted from the clause relating to Jesus' resurrection 'from the dead'; this actually moves nearer to a literal rendering of the Greek and Latin. Various Churches have followed independently the Lutheran usage of 'the holy Christian Church,' or have said 'Christ's holy Church'; and some have attempted to retranslate by saying 'the holy universal Church.'

Within American Protestantism only the Episcopal and Lutheran Churches, among the major denominations, now have the Apostles' Creed as a mandatory part of their services. The Protestant Episcopal Church permits, but seldom practises, the substitution of the Nicene Creed for the Apostles' in Morning and Evening Prayer, and also of the Apostles' Creed for the Nicene in the service of Holy Communion. It seems clear that use of the Creed is officially encouraged in Presbyterianism, but that it cannot be said to be required.

The most recent Methodist revision provides for an 'affirmation of faith' in three of its four regular orders of worship, and prints the text of the Apostles' Creed (with the modifications noted above) in the second of these. The Creed stands also in the Wesley Sunday Service, which after long neglect has been restored to the official book, as 'Order of Worship IV,' and is 'suggested for occasional use.' This compares with the previous inclusion of the Creed in a single standard order of worship, though set within brackets to indicate permissible omission; while the longer Wesley service was not published nor even mentioned. The Creed 'or some other of the authorized affirmations of faith' is also suggested for use in the Holy Communion, after the reading of the Gospel; and it has been added, without authority to omit, to the Order for the Dedication of a Church.

In the nature of their polity the Congregationally organized Churches have left the question of all Creeds entirely to the local congregations; and in general credal statements have been conspicuous by their absence from services (both published and actual) of these groups. It may be significant, however, that *The Pilgrim Hymnal,* the official Congregational book of hymns and services, which in its edition of 1931 did not include the text of the Apostles' Creed at all, now (edition of 1935) offers it as one of the possible selections in a 'third order of worship.' In the *Inter-Church Hymnal,* whose 'Aids to Worship' were edited by the distinguished Congregationalist Albert W. Palmer, the Apostles' Creed appears as the first of no less than twenty-five 'Confessions of Faith,' ancient and modern. Here the text is that of the traditional English rendering, save that 'he descended into hell' is omitted.

These Protestant variations both in the phrasing and in the use of the Creed cannot be said to be alien to the historic practice of the Church. As we have seen, the Creed gradually took form by just such processes of adjustment, and no single text ever received more than incidental and rather casual authentication in the Church's usage. At the same time, the problem of the Creed scarcely is to be solved by occasional chivvying at the details of its text. To omit 'he descended into hell,' or to avoid the supposedly difficult English words 'Ghost' and 'Catholic,' is by no means to dispose of all the problems which the Creed poses to the modern Christian. It is not by rewriting the Creed, but by interpreting it, that the Church of today may find it possible rightly to use its words and richly to apprehend its meaning. It is precisely toward an effort at interpretation that this book is directed.

3. 'GOD THE FATHER ALMIGHTY'

*'I believe in God the Father Almighty, maker of heaven
and earth.'*—The Apostles' Creed.
'No man hath seen God at any time.'—St. John 1:18(AV).
*'If anyone, having seen God, understood what he saw, he
did not see him, but some one of his creatures that are
and are known.'*—'Dionysius the Areopagite,' about
A.D. 500.[1]
*'Lord means a lot of things, I guess, but I guess all the
things it means are good.'*—William Saroyan, A.D.
1943.[2]

In the hectic summer of 1934 three Communists were convicted of vagrancy in the municipal court of San Francisco.
Actually they were convicted not because they were vagrants:
they all had regular jobs, and each had put up $1000 bail. They
were accused because their economic and political views were
unpopular. But finally they were convicted, most of the observers agreed, because in their trial before a typical middle-
class jury one of them, the girl in the group, had proclaimed
loudly that she was an 'atheist.'

The conviction was reversed on appeal to the Superior Court,
and the three defendants were set free. Between the two court
proceedings I talked with Eleanor (that was not her name), and
challenged her wisdom in thus needlessly stirring up prejudice
against herself. She replied with the standard Marxist declaration to the effect that capitalist courts always should be used
as sounding-boards for the whole of Communist doctrine. I
shifted my ground then, and asked her just what she had meant
when she called herself an 'atheist.'

'I meant that I don't believe in God.'

'What kind of God is it that you don't believe in?' I persisted.
It turned out, as I had rather supposed, that she didn't think
there was a grandfatherly gentleman sitting on a heavenly

throne, watching mankind through a supernatural telescope, and now and then interfering to direct matters more nearly to his own satisfaction.

'Do you think the universe makes sense?' I asked Eleanor. 'Do you think effect follows cause regularly enough so that we can count upon it and plan by it?'

'Of course I do.' (She had to say that, or her whole Marxist scheme of argument would have collapsed.)

'Does it seem to you,' I went on, 'that this kind of sensible universe may have been planned and set going by a conscious intelligence?'

'Why,' she said, 'it must have been.'

'Well, if you're confident of that,' I told her, 'you're much surer of your belief in God than are a lot of the clergymen and professors of theology that I know.'

We have observed that 'believing is not seeing,' that the realms of knowledge and of faith are distinct and mutually exclusive, that one's attitude toward the Creed must be founded on choice because it cannot be based on proof. No other passage in the Creed is so necessarily in the realm of faith, so inevitably beyond the reach of knowledge, as is this first sentence which deals with God. Our first postulate in this chapter must be that whatever we believe about God we do *believe*, we do not *know*.

This distinction does not excuse us, however, from the obligation to think about the question. Eleanor's atheism was intellectually disreputable not because her conclusion was negative, but because she had jumped to her conclusion without treading any path of serious enquiry and thought. She was, therefore, not entitled to voice an intellectual opinion in the field. Neither is any one of us who is unwilling to enquire and to think.

The realms of faith and of knowledge indeed are separate, but they are not and cannot be mutually contradictory. What we believe does not depend upon data and logic; but to believe what data deny and what logic disproves is to exhibit not faith but hopeless credulity. In the limited areas of information and reason, information and reason must prevail. Uncritical belief in God and uncritical atheism are equally absurd, equally unworthy of an honest and competent mind. This then becomes a second premise: that what we do believe about God, or what we do not believe about him, becomes significant for us and for others only in direct ratio to the honesty and the energy with which we have faced the intellectual problems that are involved.

This chapter will not attempt a chronological survey of historic ideas about God, though each reader would be profited if some time he would make such a study for himself. In a very real sense this whole book is about God, since it is about one series of human efforts to find and to express divine values. More specifically in the matter of our Christian belief in God the Father Almighty, I shall submit now three brief lists: a first list of things which it may be assumed a modern Christian does not believe about God; a second list of things that of necessity are in areas of doubt and question; and (after a new introduction and a shift of point of view) a third list of positive affirmations which an honest, intelligent citizen of our modern world may find himself able to make with assurance.

First, then: what do we not believe about God? (1) We do not believe that God has a physical body. (2) We do not believe that he lives in a geographical place called 'heaven'—nor, if we are to be carefully technical, in a cosmographical place either. (3) We do not believe that God has been seen with physical eyes, that his voice has been heard with physical ears, by anyone at any time in history. (4) We do not believe that ever God singled out any one nation as his special *protégé*, to be favored arbitrarily at the expense of other peoples. (5) We do not believe that God intervenes to interrupt or to counteract the natural processes of cause and effect, either at his own whim or because anyone has exerted pressure on him. (6) We do not believe that God insists on our exact obeying of a set of formal rules which he has dictated, and which he loves with all the jealous pride of personal authorship.

These six negatives need little elaboration. In a Copernican universe there is no room for a physical heaven, and so there is no location available to a physically conditioned deity. This being so, there is no way in which God can be apprehended directly by the physical senses of men and women. Nor is there room in our moral universe for divine favoritism, divine whimsicality, divine pettiness. It is true that many have thought otherwise, and among them quite possibly some of the writers of the Apostles' Creed. At these points we do not think with them, and cannot.

It will occur to the reader that negatives of this sort have supplied precisely the basis for what many people in the past few centuries have thought to be 'atheism' on their own part. It was a healthy impulse that led to the rejection of the physically inconceivable and the morally unworthy. When the Church has tried to defend its faith by continuing to assert the untenable, it has served neither God, itself, nor mankind at large. Frank recognition of the necessary 'no' is the first requirement for the discovery of any meaningful 'yes.'

The question still remains as to whether the repudiating of childish notions about God is necessarily a rejection of God himself. Actually, the negatives which we have noted are so obvious that they have little bearing on the issue. With them cleared out of the way, we are ready to turn to those considerations which matter: and these are considerations in which scientific knowledge and simple ethical judgment offer much less aid toward decision.

My second list, being one in the area of doubt, necessarily is a list of questions. These are they: (1) Is God conscious? That is, does he think? Does he experience emotion? Does he have deliberate intentions, which he proceeds deliberately to execute? (2) Is God all-powerful? Can he do always as he pleases? If he *can* do as he pleases, *does* he? Does he invariably take his own way, or does he leave real options to humanity? (3) Is God accessible? Is there any way of approach that will bring human beings near to him? Is there any way in which humans may influence him?

These queries require of course much more consideration than a single chapter can provide. They must have at least a paragraph each at this point:

(1) Is God conscious? Our reply to that question depends first upon our judgment as to whether consciousness can operate without a nervous system. Within our experience we know of no such instance, and therefore we may not dogmatize. For some the possibility will be thinkable, for others quite inconceivable. Whichever we may consider the more likely, all of us must concede that no one of us knows.

(2) Is God all-powerful? The Creed says so, and so (usually without much careful thinking) the Hebrew-Christian tradition in general has assumed. Yet if this be true, moral difficulties at once present themselves. Does God indeed create evil as well as good, as the second Isaiah once flatly says? [3] If not, does God permit evil? Or is there something in the universe itself which stubbornly resists the good purpose and the beneficent power of God? Finally we have to choose between thinking God all-good and considering him almighty. The factor of human free will helps somewhat: if one can believe in free will. But human free will does not dispose of what is called 'natural evil,' of horror and harm and suffering over which human choice has no kind of control.

(3) Is God accessible? Hebrew and Christian teaching have said 'Yes,' and have made this divine accessibility a cardinal element of the faith. The means of acquaintance with God have been identified in direct revelation, and/or in a book, and/or in a Church. The means of influencing God have been sought in sacrifice and in prayer. There is no objective evidence, no statistical correlation, that will either prove or disprove the

validity of these Hebrew-Christian assumptions and usages.

The areas of uncertainty thus remain uncertain. God may be personal or impersonal, almighty or limited, within our reach or beyond our reach. We shall choose, each of us, one alternate or the other in each of the pairs. Whichever we choose, however, we shall choose on faith, and not by knowledge.

Beyond the area of doubt, and surely above it, is the zone of affirmation. Before we attempt to list its elements, however, we must examine a further principle of methodology. Most of our difficulties, and most of our disputes, when we think and talk about God, arise from our failing to agree on the atmosphere in which the discussion moves. What the mystic states as faith, we commonly take him to mean as fact. What the Psalmist sings in his poetry, we with our prosy minds insist on hearing as prose.

We never shall understand each other this way; and, what matters more, we never shall approach an understanding of God this way. The theologian as theologian is important to us, for he can analyze issues and clear away confusions. But the theologian takes us only so far, and no further. The theologian, as such, cannot know, and may not allow himself to feel. When a theologian begins to feel, he is not a theologian but a poet; and it may be that, in this new capacity as poet, he may know something as well.

'No man hath seen God at any time.' If affirmations are to be made about God, they must be made by the poet and in the zone of poetry. John Scotus Erigena, in the ninth century A.D., knew and asserted this truth. 'What may be affirmed of God,' he held, 'is to be taken metaphorically; but what may be denied of him is to be taken literally.' [4] Literally up to this point we have denied, in the six negatives of our first list. Literally we have questioned, in the three queries that have been stated. Literally we can do no more. Metaphorically, poetically, we proceed now to affirm.

What is God? God is at any time, for any group and for any

person, the summation of the best that that person or group has known or dreamed. God for the primitive tale-teller was the artisan of that mechanical marvel, the living, operating human body. God for the desert-dweller was the maker of storms, the supplier of water. God for the farmers of the Fertile Crescent was the vital force that each spring brought new life from out the dead, brown earth.

God for Pheidias was the designer of beauty, and was beauty's design as well. God for Plato was the imperishable Idea, in which alone reality might consist. God for ancient Israel was the champion of the nation's cause. God for Jesus was a father, as understanding and as patient and as just as had been the carpenter Joseph of Nazareth. God for St. Paul was the redeemer of mankind from the bondage of sin and death. God for St. Francis was the creator of 'our brother the sun' and 'our sister the moon,' the friend of our humility and the gracious giver of our death.[5] God for every Christian is the eternalizing of those moral values which Christianity has found in Jesus the Christ; so that the very best we can say of God is that 'God is like the Christ in whom we believe.'

In these terms, and upon this new foundation, the intellectual questions of our second list become the moral affirmations of the third. (1) Is God conscious? Is he personal? Since conscious personality is the meaning of our life, and the giver of its meaning, personal consciousness is for us a minimum attribute of a meaningful God. God, we must say, is at least personal: he cannot be other because he cannot be less. We know God as person in every person who has meaning for us; and in these persons we may not deny God's personality. 'Some one of his creatures that are and are known,' says he who writes as Dionysius. 'Our sons who have shown us God,' wrote the late H. G. Wells in the last line of *Mr. Britling Sees It Through.* Literally, we have no way of knowing whether God is conscious. Morally, we know God as person because we know God in the persons he has created.

(2) Is God almighty? If God be our highest good, and if we believe that good can prevail, must prevail, therefore shall prevail: I say 'if we believe,' for this too is a matter of faith: if thus we do believe, then we believe that God is all-powerful and is not to be defeated. We believe that beauty will triumph over ugliness, health over disease, honesty over falsehood, love over contempt and hate: right over wrong. God then is on our side, for we are on God's side. We believe then that God the Father, God the beautiful, the good, and the true, is God Almighty indeed.

(3) Is God accessible? This is the final test of such a faith, and this is its final triumph. If God be the highest good and the loveliest beauty and the realest truth, then whenever we recognize good or see beauty or find truth, we recognize and see and find God. Yet more, when we are good or beautiful or true we are God, for then we are partakers of his nature: [6] we are in God and organically a part of him. And this is how we influence God, by the prayer and the sacrifice that are our own Godlike lives. Can we know God? Can we reach him? Can we persuade him? How can we but reach and know him in all the beauty and truth and goodness we have found in this his world? How can we but persuade him as we play our part in him, in this world which is ours and his?

It has not been my habit to talk much about God. Once, I recall, I spoke at a University meeting on the subject, 'A Valid Religion for Today'; and a discerning and non-religious friend remarked afterward that I had talked for almost an hour about religion without mentioning God once. Verbally, my friend was right; but I dare to trust that God was not wholly absent from my thought and feeling about the religious life. For years I have rather deliberately avoided using the word 'God,' except historically and liturgically.[7] I have done so because I think the word for many hearers is meaningless, and for some is positively confusing and misleading, in view of the great variety of conceptions and misconceptions attaching to it.

I do not expect greatly to alter my verbal habit. It is not the word 'God,' but the experience of God, that matters: and the experience is by no necessity confined within the limits of the word. It appears from the Gospel records, especially those in the historically more dependable Gospels according to St. Mark, St. Matthew, and St. Luke, that Jesus talked about God surprisingly little. It appears that Jesus did two things much more important: he discovered God in his own heart, and he revealed God in his own life. 'No man hath seen God at any time.' That text as previously quoted herein is incomplete. The sentence goes on: 'The only-begotten son, who is in the bosom of the Father, he hath revealed him.'

What is 'God the Father Almighty'? Who is he? God is the one supreme value for the nation of Israel, and for all the nations of men. God is one whom no man has seen at any time, and whom no man can understand save in 'some one of his creatures that are and are known.' God is for us the meaning of the person of Jesus, and of the mission of the Christ. God is poetry. God is spirit. God is life. 'Lord means a lot of things, I guess, (and) I guess all the things it means are good.' If we believe them good: if we believe in the good as real and living, as compelling and victorious: then we do 'believe in God the Father Almighty, maker of heaven and earth.'

4. 'HIS ONLY SON OUR LORD'

'Who do men say that I am? And they told him, saying, John the Baptist; and others, Elijah; but others, One of the prophets. And he asked them, But who say ye that I am? Peter answereth and saith unto him, Thou art the Christ.'—St. Mark 8:27–30 (ARV).[1]

'Let all the house of Israel therefore know assuredly, that God hath made him both Lord and Christ, this Jesus whom ye crucified.'—Acts 2:36 (ARV).

'And in Jesus Christ his only Son our Lord: Who was conceived by the Holy Ghost, Born of the Virgin Mary: Suffered under Pontius Pilate, Was crucified, dead, and buried: He descended into hell; The third day he rose again from the dead: He ascended into heaven, And sitteth on the right hand of God the Father Almighty: From thence he shall come to judge the quick and the dead.'—The Apostles' Creed.

Of the total of 110 words of the English text of the Apostles' Creed, 70 are in the paragraph which stands above, and which deals entirely with faith in Jesus Christ. All the other considerations in the Creed: God the Father, the Holy Ghost, the Church, the forgiveness of sins, the life everlasting: all these are mentioned, as it were, by title only; but the Christian view of Jesus is presented with some elaboration of detail.

The next several chapters will be devoted to enquiry into the details, each in its turn. This one will attempt a consideration of the person and character of Jesus the Christ, by raising four questions which naturally occur to almost every mind, four questions with which inescapably we have to deal. Phrased as briefly and directly as our language will allow, they are: (1) Was Jesus? (2) Was Jesus a man? (3) Was the Christ a god? (4) Is the Christ? The first of these four queries is strictly historical: did Jesus live? The second and third are interpretive: our own putting of the question which the Gospels ascribe to him, 'Who say ye that I am?' The fourth is experiential: what

29

reality has this Jesus, called the Christ, for us who name his name?

Number one: Was Jesus? Did Jesus live? Two extremes of opinion here are to be noticed. On the one side, those who are called 'fundamentalists' hold that the four Gospels in our New Testament are strictly accurate records of factual detail, presenting exactly what happened at all points. On the other hand, some self-styled 'rationalists' contend that Jesus is a purely imaginary figure, for whose historic life there is no evidence at all.[2] Neither of these extremes is tenable in the light of the knowledge that is within our reach.

We must note that the Gospel documents are far from being eyewitness or even contemporary records of Jesus' life; that at many points they are internally as well as mutually contradictory; that they exhibit propaganda interests which forbid our acceptance of them as accurate, objective reporting. The Gospels are portraits rather than photographs. They say much about Jesus; but what really they tell us about is the thinking of their authors and their first readers.

We are not permitted, then, to cite the Gospels as if they were, or as if they contained, precise statements of external fact. In particular we are not justified in using quotations from them with the introductory formula, 'Jesus said:' The legitimate way of treatment is indicated in such phrasings as 'St. Matthew's Gospel represents that . . .'; 'St. Luke's Gospel quotes Jesus as saying . . .' The Gospels are important and authoritative source materials for our knowledge of the developing Christian tradition. They are secondary authorities, and as to specific detail undependable authorities, for the career of Jesus of Nazareth.

It does not follow that we must leap to the opposite extreme of complete denial. The Gospels are not better authorities than are many other biographical writings of the ancient world, but they are scarcely worse than most. The old gossip Suetonius wrote a lot of rather scandalous fiction about the Roman emperors; but that does not mean that the emperors themselves are fictitious personages. Tacitus recorded the reign of Nero with a strong propaganda bias, without driving anyone to the conclusion that there never was a Nero. Closer to our own time, Parson Weems indulged in rhapsodic fairy tales about George Washington. We still are of the opinion that there was a Washington. It was not General Pershing, but the comparatively little known Charles E. Stanton, who said 'Lafayette, we are here.' That does not wipe out the General's military record.

On the whole, it is more reasonable to believe that there was a Galilean teacher named Jesus (or, more strictly, Joshua, which is nearer to the original Semitic form of the name); a teacher who lived substantially the kind of life that the Gospels present: than to argue that his figure was created out of whole cloth by the very diverse men who wrote the books which have come to us. The very discrepancies and contradictions strengthen the case for an original, central reality from which all the accounts have moved in their several different directions. A purely fictional figure surely would have been more carefully planned, more consistently portrayed, than is this hero of faith of whom we catch occasional glimpses through the words that have been written about him.

Was Jesus? We have reason to think he was. Sober historical judgment supports the view that he lived in Palestine, that he taught a modified but revitalized Judaism, that he was executed because he seemed dangerous to the established order of things. More importantly, sober historical judgment also suggests that Jesus taught with such clarity, lived with such intensity, that he shook those who knew him into ways of thinking and living that for them were new and different: and that therefore he himself could not but become, for them, the center of a new religious cult. That cult, which later came to be called 'Christianity,' thought about its hero, and kept on rethinking: and in its thinking about him produced both the four Gospels and our seventy-word formula in the Creed. Was Jesus? We may conclude that he was.

What was he? This leads to question number two: Was Jesus a man? Today's thought habits would lead us to say, 'Of course. If he was at all, he had to be a man. What else could he be?'

Greco-Roman antiquity did not think in quite the same way. It was readier to find inspiration in a god than in a human being. It was far enough from modern laboratory techniques not to worry much about questions of scientific demonstration. Actually the first heresies that arose within the Christian group were those which denied not the divinity of the Christ, but the humanity of Jesus.

Detailed study of the Gospel records indicates that Jesus was a man indeed, and that he was so considered by his contemporaries. For thirty years he seems to have lived a fairly normal life as a Galilean villager. For a little less than three years, apparently, he was active in a fairly usual and familiar way as a Jewish traveling teacher of religion. At the end of that time, we gather, he died the death normally expected for anyone who was crucified on a Roman cross.

The first Palestinian followers of Jesus never doubted his genuine humanity, and neither has the majority view of the Christian Church at any time in history. But Greeks who had not known Jesus, and who in general were disposed to deprecate all that was physical and objective, increasingly subordinated the historic data to their interests in philosophical interpretation and in mystical feeling. The Gospels and the Creed alike reflect both of these contrary and conflicting trends of thought, the Palestinian and the Greek, and in their surviving texts they exhibit many elements of the controversies that arose.

The earliest stratum of Gospel narrative, that collection of the reported sayings of Jesus which is quoted at length in the Gospels according to St. Matthew and St. Luke, contains neither claims nor episodes of what we would call a 'supernatural' kind.

The earliest complete Gospel, that according to St. Mark, asserts numerous limitations both upon Jesus' knowledge and upon his power. But the later strands in St. Matthew and St. Luke, and almost the entire text of the still later Gospel attributed to St. John, emphasize the extraordinary and the supra-human at the expense of normal human quality.

Within the Church the denial of the human nature of Jesus proceeded apace. About A.D. 200 St. Clement of Alexandria declared:

As to the savior, it would be absurd to think that the body required, as a body, the ordinary necessities for survival: for he ate not for the sake of the body, which was held together by holy power, but so that his associates should not think otherwise concerning him.[3]

Thus for this Alexandrian Platonist the human appearance of the historic Jesus was quite deceptive, and was merely a concession to the intellectual and spiritual dullness of the disciples. The teachers who called themselves 'Gnostic,' claiming to know special, hidden truth, went beyond the Virgin Birth doctrine to argue that Jesus derived nothing even from a human mother, but that he had come through Mary into the world 'like water passing through a tube.'[4] Nestorius denied the union of human with divine nature in Jesus, Apollinaris asserted that Jesus was absolute God in a temporary physical, human disguise.

Both these elements, the human and the divine, are represented in the Creed as we have it. On the side of normal humanity, explicitly and deliberately asserted in reply to such teachings as those of the Gnostics, are the personal, then ordinary name, 'Jesus' (which, as we have noted, is the Greco-Latin form of the Semitic 'Joshua'); the reference to the human mother, Mary; and the detailed review of actual suffering under the Roman Pilate, of actual crucifixion, death, and burial. On the side of supra-human divinity are the terms 'Christ' and 'only Son our Lord,' the reference to divine fatherhood through the Holy Ghost, and the allusions to the resurrection, the ascension, the second coming, and the final judgment. On this deifying side too there should perhaps be counted the total omission from the Creed of any reference to Jesus' teaching ministry, probably due in part to that pull away from external fact which was influencing all the members of the growing Church.

Was Jesus of Nazareth indeed a man? If he lived at all among men, he must have been. The first three Gospels portray him as growing, learning, contending, suffering, being defeated: all of which are universal human experiences. If those experiences were not actual in Jesus' case, Jesus himself could mean but little to growing and contending and suffering and defeated mankind. Historical good sense and moral necessity unite to insist upon the genuine human nature, and the genuine human experience, of the historic Jesus of Nazareth. And so to our second question, 'Was Jesus a man?,' we answer positively, 'Yes.'

What kind of man was he? The answer which the Church made sets the stage for question number three: 'Was the Christ a god?' At this point we must note the importance of drawing a very definite line between the two words 'Jesus' and 'Christ.' 'Jesus' is the personal name of an individual, probably historic, at a given point in time. 'Christ' is an idea which has a history much older than 'Jesus,' and also much more recent. 'Jesus' represents a historical datum. 'Christ' involves the expression of a judgment. As applied to Jesus, the word 'Christ' specifically states an opinion about him.

The term always should be used with the definite article, '*The* Christ.' Our word is the Greek *ho Christos,* which is a translation of the Hebrew *ha-mashiach,* by us read as 'the Messiah.' 'The Messiah' and 'the Christ,' translated instead of transliterated, both mean 'the anointed one.' In Jewish tradition they refer to the expected national hero who should deliver the nation of Judah from alien oppression: oppression which had been successively Assyrian, Babylonian, Persian, Greek, Syrian, Roman. In Christian usage 'the Christ' means that Jesus was by the early Jewish Christians identified as being this deliverer in person.

This was the first step taken toward making Jesus divine. While the functions of the Jewish Messiah were conceived as being military and political, his character often and increasingly was represented as supernatural. Those parts of our Creed which predict the 'second coming' and the 'last judgment' derive immediately from Jewish Messianic ideas and teachings. They assign to Jesus the character and the activities which belong to the Jewish Messiah: overthrowing the existing regime, and passing judgment upon mankind. Obviously Jesus had not been at all this sort of person, and had not done at all this sort of thing, during his life in Palestine. Once his followers had thought to identify him as 'the Christ,' and promptly had encountered Jewish objections to the effect that Jesus had performed no such Messianic functions, they developed the theory that Jesus would be the expected spectacular Messiah in a future career upon the earth.

This whole Jewish thought-world was quite alien and meaningless to the Greeks who soon came to be the majority within the Christian fellowship. Jewish nationalism held no real importance for the Greek Jew, Saul of Tarsus, who as the apostle St. Paul was to become the most vital single force in determining the Christian standards of faith and life. While St. Paul used the term 'Christ,' he rather frequently dropped the definite article from before it; and therein reflected what indeed was the fact: that in his mind the word 'Christ' was a name rather than a title.[5]

What St. Paul thought of his 'Christ' was something entirely different. Negatively oriented as to Jewish national concerns, positively influenced by the prevailing religious patterns of the Mediterranean world, St. Paul found in Jesus Christ the redeemer not from national tragedy but from personal, the savior not of a community from Roman oppression but of the individual from the power of sin and death. This redemption, this salvation, St. Paul assigned to the death of Jesus, conceived as a sacrificial

offering. By symbolic sharing in this sacrifice the believer himself was raised from the death of sin to the life of righteousness.
Thus from the religion of Jesus, a simple ethical pattern on the
Jewish model, standard Christianity became a religion about
the Christ, a complex mystical experience of Greco-Oriental
character. The Galilean teacher had been assimilated to, if not
wholly transformed into, a Hellenistic god.

Instead of trying at this point to answer question number
three: 'Was the Christ really a god?,' let us pass now to number
four: 'Is the Christ?' Our judgment as to whether St. Paul and
the Church were right in ascribing special divine quality to
the founder and the center of their faith depends necessarily
upon our own decision as to whether we can discern such quality
in him.

Our reply has to be a dual one. First, we must recognize that
the Church never could have arrived at such a judgment had
there not been in the historic figure something which human
observers identified as unique, as so specially important that
they could not describe it otherwise than as being divine. The
resurrection of Jesus, to take a crucial point for example, is
conditioned directly upon the persisting power of his life in
the memory of those who had known him. 'For these who loved
him, he could never die.' [6]

Second, we are driven to observe that the Christ indeed is, is
valid and meaningful, is savior from sin and redeemer from
moral destruction, for all who find him thus to be: and this
quite independently, in logic and in experience alike, of all
consideration of the historical Jesus. Again it is truth, not fact,
which chiefly matters. We are concerned the less with fact which
we must try to disentangle, the more with truth toward which
we may learn to rise.

This finally is what the Creed tells us. Those statements about
Jesus the Christ which are the easier for us to accept, those of
the simple historical narrative, are precisely the less important

ones for Christian faith. The difficult declarations, those which assert the eternal reality of the living Lord, are the crucial elements of continuing Christian experience. The Church had found God in Jesus, and so it called Jesus 'the Christ'; and later, under the influence of Greek thought-forms, 'the only-begotten Son' of God.

The Christ, the Son of God, as the Church came to believe in him, was and is real in power and in beauty and in goodness, and so was and is real in truth. Nineteen Christian centuries bear witness to this reality. The crucified Lord, who died that men might live, is our persisting and undying symbol of sacrificial love. The risen savior is our expression of the glory of being, of the promise that life can have meaning beyond the moment, that it can know triumph beyond despair. The eternal judge of the living and the dead is himself the standard by which we test the quality of our own living.

The Jesus of history is the point at which Christianity started. The grave mistake which American 'modernist' Christology has made is not in its recognizing of this indisputable fact. It is in its supposing that the Jesus of history is not only beginning, but also end. Historically the distinction between the first-century Jesus and the eternal Christ is helpful because it clarifies origins. Morally and theologically the distinction is misleading, and destructive, when it is used to discredit the concept of the Christ in its concern for the personality of Jesus.

The Jesus of history is not the whole Christ for us, and cannot be. We know more, of our own experience, about the Christ of faith. In our experience we know the Christ of faith at first hand. This Christ of faith is the ideal which man finds, not alone in reading records of the past, but also and vitally in facing the total challenge of his own life.

The Church called Jesus divine because it had found him to be like God. We know no better way to describe God than to say he must be like our Christ. The Church created her Christ out of the data of fact and the splendor of dreams. We are entitled not only to believe in the Christ. We are permitted, we are challenged, continuingly to create our Christ: to see him grow for us still finer and greater than ever he was before, as our own experience is the more richly charged with meaning.

'No man hath seen God at any time.' What we have seen of God in this our world: what yet we shall see of him incarnate in humanity: this is our Christ. This is for us God's Son: 'His only Son our Lord.' Jesus was. The Christ is. How truly for us, it is for us to decide.

5. 'BORN OF THE VIRGIN MARY'

'Conceived by the Holy Ghost, Born of the Virgin Mary.'
—The Apostles' Creed.
*'The Holy Ghost shall come upon thee, and the power of
the Highest shall overshadow thee: therefore also that
holy thing which shall be born of thee shall be called
the Son of God.'*—St. Luke 1:35 (AV).
*'When we declare that the Word, who is the first-born of
God, came into being without sexual intercourse . . .
we do not report anything different from your view
about those called sons of Zeus.'*—St. Justin Martyr,
about A.D. 150.[1]
*'The Spirit itself beareth witness with our spirit, that we
are the children of God: and if children, then heirs;
heirs of God, and joint-heirs with Christ.'*—Romans
8:17 (AV).

'Born of the Virgin Mary' may not be ultimately the most
difficult phrase in the Apostles' Creed. For most of us, however,
it is almost certainly the first to give trouble. To our minds it
seems improbable in itself that anyone should be born without
a human father; and so as soon as we begin to ask questions for
ourselves, we put one of our biggest question marks beside this
statement. Was Jesus born of the Virgin Mary? What evidence
is there for the truth of this item as set forth?

The question of evidence we shall come to soon, and shall
dwell on at some length. But before we do that, we must notice
first that the question of evidence is not the really important one.
Much more significant than the issue of whether Jesus actually
was born of a virgin, is the problem of why people thought he
was, of what they meant when they said he was. Frankly, I
would not consider devoting so much as a full chapter to the
Virgin Birth if I thought that either the establishing or the
denial of its factuality was the essential point. In that case I
would simply remark that the evidence we have is not such as to

convince any reasonable mind, and so that belief in the Virgin Birth is without proper foundation.

Indeed, it is precisely because the evidence for the Virgin Birth as fact is hopelessly weak, that the doctrine of the Virgin Birth becomes worth our careful study. The next few paragraphs will attempt to summarize the evidence as it stands. Granting at the outset that it is unconvincing, I suggest that the existence of the doctrine, in default of good evidence, indicates that something other than factual evidence is at stake. It is not whether the Birth from a Virgin happened that concerns us. What matters is why Christian people came to say that it had happened.

With that premise in mind, let us look now at the factual evidence. To begin with, we must notice that there is no word about the Virgin Birth in the writings of St. Paul, whose authentic letters are the earliest parts of our New Testament; that there is no mention of the Virgin Birth in St. Mark's Gospel, the first-written and the most nearly factual of the four; and that there is no allusion to the Virgin Birth in St. John's Gospel, which among all the accounts of Jesus lays the greatest stress upon his divine character. That is to say, all these major documents of early Christianity present faith in Jesus as the Christ without making the slightest reference to his parentage. It would seem reasonably to follow that these writers either never had heard of the doctrine, or that they thought it wholly unimportant.

Where then does the doctrine of the Virgin Birth appear? The answer, so far as the New Testament is concerned, is that it appears in two Gospels: those named for St. Matthew and St. Luke. To be more exact, we must say that the Virgin Birth appears in eight verses in St. Matthew, and in two verses in St. Luke: [2] and nowhere else in either of the books. Moreover, each of these Gospels which does contain the statement of Mary's virginity also contains statements and inferences which tend to deny it. Most notably, each of them presents a genealogy for Jesus; and each traces Jesus' ancestry not through Mary at all, but through Joseph. It is true that in each case a phrase has been inserted in an attempt to straighten things out: in St. Matthew, after Joseph's name, 'the husband of Mary, of whom was born Jesus,' and in St. Luke the expression 'being the son (as was supposed) of Joseph.' [3] But aside from the obvious awkwardness of these adjustments, the fact remains that no one conceivably would have bothered to trace Jesus' descent down through the generations to Joseph, unless he assumed that Joseph indeed was Jesus' father; and so that the genealogies must have been compiled by people who had no notion other than that Jesus was Joseph's son.

Some have tried to defend the Virgin Birth on the ground that it was predicted centuries before by the prophet Isaiah; and the editor of St. Matthew's Gospel makes eager use of this argument.[4] Unhappily for such a view, it is without foundation in the book of Isaiah itself. Had our Gospel editor been reading the original Hebrew instead of a Greek mistranslation made quite innocently by the Jews of Alexandria, he would have found no 'virgin' in the passage at all. What Isaiah said to the king Ahaz was not, 'A virgin shall conceive,' but 'The young woman is pregnant'; and he was talking about a young woman of that time, about B.C. 735, not at all of one to be born more than seven hundred years later. One need not belabor the point that we do no honor to our Christian faith by trying to defend it through the use of mistaken translations of our documents.

Actually, we can cut the Virgin Birth sections from both our Gospels without doing any violence to the flow of the narrative. In the case of St. Luke, the story makes appreciably more sense without the Virgin Birth element. As the account stands, the archangel Gabriel promises that Mary will have a son of extraordinary quality; and she responds by saying that she cannot understand this, since she is a virgin. But it has been made clear that Mary already was engaged to Joseph; and so her normal reaction to the angel's promise surely would be to assume that the son was to be born in due course after the marriage. Mary's reply thus is unconvincing, and the narrative is more intelligible if these two verses are simply left out.

It thus becomes clear, not only that most of the New Testament gets along perfectly well without the Virgin Birth, but also that the Virgin Birth does not really belong in the material where it now does stand. In other words, the doctrine of the Virgin Birth of Jesus does not derive from the New Testament at all, but was introduced into it from some other source. Our next enquiry therefore must be into the possible sources from which the idea may have come.

The answer is not far to seek. It is expressed perfectly clearly by St. Justin the Martyr, in the sentence from his *First Apology* which stands at the head of this chapter, and which in its original context is supported by numerous illustrations from pagan mythology. Within the Greek thought-world, the appearance among men of an extraordinary person was explained, almost as a matter of course, by saying that he had a father who was more than human. Thus did the Greeks account for the strength of Heracles, and the heroism of Perseus, and the exploits of Bellerophon. It was wholly natural, indeed it was almost inevitable, that the early Christians in a Greek community, trying to assert the special character of their Christ, should use this accepted and familiar formula with reference to his origin.

Here we must remind ourselves that the ancient world had no such notions of causation, of physical limitation, as we laboratory-trained moderns take for granted. It is almost strictly accurate to say that it was not the ordinary, but the extraordinary, that first-century people found it the easiest to believe. There was so much in their world that for them was beyond explanation, that the few apparently explainable things tended to drop into unimportance; and value thus attached chiefly to the myriad wonders that everyone felt everywhere about him.

It was for such reasons as this that the first Christian heresy: that is to say, the first major departure from the central Christian tradition: was not at all a denying that the Christ was divine, but was specifically a denying that Jesus had been human. Not only recognized heretics, but also many of the orthodox Christian leaders, came soon to believe that Jesus had had no genuine physical body, that he had needed no food for his sustenance, that he could not have suffered actual physical pain upon the cross. In such an atmosphere, it was the easiest possible thing to say that Jesus had come into the world by other than the ordinary means of procreation.

An examination of the early manuscripts of St. Luke's Gospel shows that it was the Gnostic heretic Tatian who first changed 'his father and his mother' (in St. Luke 2:33) to read 'Joseph and his mother,' thus adjusting the primitive account to the later doctrine.[5] That is to say, a phrase which indicated an early assumption of Jesus' human parentage was altered so as to conform to the theory of the Virgin Birth; and was altered precisely on the initiative of one of those heretical teachers whose principal concern was to deny the true human nature of Jesus of Nazareth. It would be too much to argue that the whole doctrine of the Virgin Birth was created by such heretics. But we may reasonably say that it did arise in the thought-world to which both the orthodox and the heretics belonged, and that it expressed from the outset just that deprecation of the natural and the ordinary which all first-century people held in common.

The developing other-worldliness of Christianity, based largely upon the idea that Jesus soon would return from heaven to wind up all earthly affairs, worked together with this Greek dualism to make the whole matter of sexual relations seem unworthy of a religious view of life. To this day, in the technical phrasing of the Catholic Church, a 'religious' person is a monastic, a celibate. At this point the doctrine of the Virgin Birth may become not merely an incidental matter, but a very real danger. If ever it is understood to mean that the normal way of continuing the human family is in itself unworthy, it becomes a denial of the validity of normal human life. Now and then sexuality has been a menace to religion; but scarcely more of a menace than has existed in certain kinds of anti-sexuality. Whatever else the doctrine of the Virgin Birth may mean or may not mean to us, we must not permit it to bring into disrepute what can be one of the most beautiful and most significant elements of human experience. Whatever else the doctrine may mean, to us it may not mean that God's way of creating men is unworthy either of man or of God.

It is important that we should notice here just what the original nature of our doctrine was. Later in the same work from which I have quoted, St. Justin seems to contradict himself. In the 21st chapter of his *First Apology,* as we have seen, St. Justin says that the birth of Jesus is exactly comparable to the birth of the sons of Zeus. In the 33rd chapter, however, he insists that Mary remained a virgin,[6] and so that her case was different from those of Leda, Danae, and the other mothers of the Greek heroes. This latter view ultimately became standard in the Church; but certainly it is not supported by most of the early authorities.

It is difficult to read the phrasing in St. Luke:

The Holy Ghost shall come upon thee, and the power of the Highest shall overshadow thee: therefore also that holy thing which shall be born of thee shall be called the Son of God,

with any meaning other than that God, in the form of the Holy Ghost, is to take the place of the human father. In his letter to the Ephesians St. Ignatius speaks of the 'one physician' as 'both from Mary and from God.'[7] As we noted above, the fourth-century Marcellus of Ancyra, almost three hundred years after St. Luke's Gospel reached its final editing, still used the phrasing 'born of the Holy Ghost and Mary the Virgin.'[8] Since Marcellus was trying to establish his own Christian orthodoxy, we must assume that what he said did not seem to him to conflict with the orthodox views of his time. And to try to make his expression mean anything other than that the Holy Ghost and Mary the Virgin were the two parents of Jesus is to deny the plain meaning of his words.[9]

Let us summarize the results of our enquiry thus far. First, the doctrine of the Virgin Birth appears to have been unknown to most New Testament writers, and is clearly an intrusion into those writings in which it does appear. Second, the doctrine fits exactly into the prevailing pattern of Mediterranean thought about the parentage of great men. Third, the original form of the doctrine was not that of a Virgin Birth properly so called, what the biologists would describe as 'parthenogenesis,' but rather that of the birth of Jesus from a human mother and a divine father.

Since the evidence is historically weak, since the frame of reference is not one that we can accept, the question of fact disposes of itself. No sober historian can assert that the Virgin Birth occurred, and no reasonable modern thinker will argue that the Virgin Birth is necessary to explain Jesus. Those who do so assert are bad historians, those who try thus to explain are poor philosophers. In these cold and literal terms, then, we do not believe in the Virgin Birth.

Is this all that there is to be said? I have urged that, if it be, the issue is not worth the space of a single chapter. Is it possible nevertheless to justify so much discussion of the problem?

Actually, disposing of the doctrine historically, and/or philosophically, has no effect at all upon the foundation on which the doctrine first was based. Why did people say that Jesus was born of a Virgin? For one reason, and one only: namely, that he was so extraordinary a person that ordinary backgrounds seemed for him quite inadequate. The character of Jesus stands out, quite separately from this ancient attempt at explaining it, and surviving that attempt without loss of any kind. We shall not try to account for Jesus' moral uniqueness by a theory of biological uniqueness; but the moral uniqueness of Jesus stands, and still defies our own attempts at its explaining.

As time went on, and Christian thought was developed in more detail, the theory of the Virgin Birth of Jesus came to be used in connection with the doctrine of original sin. Because Jesus had no human father, went the argument, he escaped the sinful heritage of Adam, and so was free from the taint which all men else had inherited. Soon, however, the logical fallacy here became apparent. After all, Mary as well as Joseph was understood to be descended from Adam and Eve; and so, if Jesus was Mary's son, he inherited Adam's sinfulness no less truly than if he had been Joseph's son as well.

To get rid of this difficulty some Christian thinkers worked out another theory: this time one not of a biological miracle, but of a theological one. They began to say that, at the time of the conception of Mary, nine months before her birth, God interposed to remove the taint of original sin from that embryo. This doctrine is known as that of the 'Immaculate Conception.' Of course it never should be confused, as so often it has been, with that of the Virgin Birth itself. The dogma of the 'Immaculate Conception' ultimately became official in Roman Catholic doctrine, though not until the year 1854. It never has been accepted by any Protestant body. Yet it remains logically necessary, if the sinlessness of Jesus is at all to be based upon the question of who his parent or parents may have been.[10]

Here again we are dealing with a series of assumptions that are not our own, and that therefore have no real meaning for us. The sinfulness of man we find not in our ancestors, but in ourselves; not in theories of origin, but in facts of observation. If on examination of the record we conclude that Jesus was sinless, we shall do so on the ground that we do not find him to have been a sinner. Morally, to give him a supernatural advantage at the outset is to rob his asserted freedom from sin of all real meaning; for if Jesus could not sin, his not sinning had no merit and offers us no hope. We know we can sin, we know we have sinned. The question remains whether we can conquer sin; and it is a truly human Jesus, not an arbitrarily supernatural one, whose example alone can encourage us to share in his moral triumph.

In point of fact, the early Christians held eagerly and strongly to faith in Jesus' real humanity. While they were so far influenced by prevailing supernaturalism as to accept the doctrine of the Virgin Birth, the major leaders of the Church repudiated indignantly the notion that Jesus derived nothing from his human mother. St. Irenaeus in the second century and St. Epiphanius in the fourth unite to condemn those heretics who taught that Jesus came into the world 'as water through a tube.' [11]

Functionally, the credal declaration that Jesus was 'born of the Virgin Mary' was understood to be not nearly so much a statement that he had no human father, as that he very positively did have a human mother.[12] As we shall see in the chapter below which attempts to discuss Jesus' suffering and death, the precise point of all these statements in the Creed about the details of Jesus' personal history is to insist upon the real character of his human experience, in defiance of those who held him to be so divine that he could not be human at all. To the members of the early Church, and so quite properly to us also, the affirmation that Jesus was 'born of the Virgin Mary' stands as the crucially important affirmation that Jesus did belong to the human family, and so that he is our brother indeed.

To speak of the family reminds us of another factor in the situation: that of the place of Mary herself. Out of the doctrine of the Virgin Birth arose the cult of the Blessed Virgin. That is one way of putting it. Another, and surely a more valid analysis, is that the cult of the Blessed Virgin rose out of man's need to recognize the woman's touch in the totality of human life. The pagan world with its many deities could take care of this easily, but Hebrew and Christian monotheism could not; and the primacy of males in ancient Israelite society had made the single Jewish God quite decisively masculine. Around the Mediterranean basin in the first century, however, were spread a number of religions which held in common tó a mother deity, to a dying and rising savior who was at once her consort and her son, and to personal salvation through the agency of these two divine beings.

Here again the general Mediterranean heritage of Christianity comes into play. As the Christian faith gained ground, the worship of Isis and Osiris in Egypt fell into disrepute. But the statues of Isis, the mother-goddess, were not destroyed. They were but rechiselled a bit, and their inscriptions changed; and thus they stood, still as representations of the womanly aspect of the divine being, though now expressed no longer in Isis, but rather in the Blessed Virgin Mary. Grace, beauty, tenderness: these seemed by right to belong to woman more than to man; and thus to bring the Virgin into the Christian scheme of things was the more easily to preserve tenderness, and beauty, and grace, in the Christian religion.

By a curious accident of the calendar, the sermon in which this chapter had its roots happened to be preached in the Mills College Chapel on the second Sunday in May of the year 1947. I understand that 'Mothers' Day,' though suggested by a woman, was first promoted by a men's fraternal order. I know that it has been continued chiefly within the framework of American Protestant Christianity. And I suggest that Mothers' Day is to be understood as a kind of Protestant substitute (perhaps not very adequate, but nonetheless real) for the adoration of Mary. As Protestants we had rejected the Catholic usage, yet still we had the common human need; and so, by indirection, we use Mothers' Day to restore Mary the mother to her place in this our honoring of all the mothers of all of us.

'Born of the Virgin Mary.' Can we still say those words in

honesty? Few of us can, in literal terms. We do not think the evidence is good, and we do not find the philosophical need compelling. Yet it may be that we can say the phrase, and with intensified because realized meaning, if we see in it those values from which both the phrase and the doctrine came. 'Born of the Virgin Mary'? This is not fact; and still for us it can be true.

It can be true if in it we read the early Christian conviction that Jesus was human in very truth, and St. Paul's assurance that we, being also children of God, may become joint-heirs with Christ. It can be true also if in this phrase we admit our recognition of what womanhood and womanliness have meant, and can mean, and should mean, to all our human brotherhood and sisterhood. It can be true for us, finally, if in it we declare anew our conviction that Jesus the Christ is for us the supreme value, whom to describe we need all the words at our command, and whom to know we must rise beyond all the words that man has known.

To honor motherhood; to know the real humanity of Jesus; to accept the primacy of the Christ: this is to share fully in what the ancient doctrine tried to say. This then is to join with the men and women of old in the essential meaning of their faith. Have we learned, in the Spirit, that we are the children of God? If we are God's children, we are heirs of God, and joint-heirs with the Christ. 'The holy thing that shall be born of thee shall be called the Son of God.' Are we God's children enough to recognize our Brother?

6. THE SURPRISING SILENCE

'Say ye of him, whom the Father hath sanctified, and sent into the world, Thou blasphemest; because I said, I am the Son of God?'—St. John 10:36 (AV).
'Last of all John, observing that the bodily things had been made known in the (other) Gospels, being urged by his friends, and inspired by the Spirit, wrote a spiritual Gospel.'—St. Clement of Alexandria, about A.D. 200.[1]

One of the chief complaints against the Creed, urged by many modern Christians, is that it has nothing whatever to say about Jesus' ministry as a teacher. From 'born of the Virgin Mary' the credal text passes immediately to 'suffered under Pontius Pilate.' There is no reference to the years in Nazareth, none to the journeys in Galilee, none to the visits in Bethany. There is no mention of the ethical challenge of Jesus' words, none of the inspiriting example of his personality. Thus, say the critics, the Creed exhausts itself wholly on the theological, if not on the magical, aspects of Christian thinking about the Lord.

Again we must admit that if we were writing the Creed today, we would not choose to be silent about what seem to us the central elements in the Gospel story. We would want to say something about the moral demands of the Sermon on the Mount, about the commandments of love to God and man, about the call to take up the cross and follow. Yet even within the framework of our own thought it is not easy to make selections for specific reference in a brief declaration of faith. Thus one of the two modern creeds which follows the Apostles' Creed in the current edition of *The Methodist Hymnal* makes no direct mention of Jesus' ministry, and the other includes it only by describing him as 'our Teacher, Example, (and Redeemer).' Similarly the numerous 'Confessions of Faith' assembled by

Albert W. Palmer in *The Inter-Church Hymnal* say actually very little of Jesus' teaching as such.[2] The fact seems to be that materials of this sort do not lend themselves readily to summary statement.

The question nevertheless requires to be answered, as to why the early Church apparently made no such attempt. (It will be realized that the Nicene Creed is equally silent about the ministry of Jesus, unless the clause 'and was made man' be understood to imply the years of human activity.) The first and decisive reply to our question is that the Creeds of necessity were directed toward matters in dispute, and not to those on which there was general agreement.

We have seen that the dominant factor in the construction of the paragraph relating to Jesus the Christ was the Church's insistence upon Jesus' real humanity. This issue centered, however, not upon the record of Jesus' teaching, but rather upon such questions as those of the reality of his human birth, his human suffering, his human death. Those parts of the Gospel narrative which stood between the birth and the arrest were not themselves in debate; for Gnostics not less than orthodox believers accepted these accounts without questioning their historicity.[3] It followed that a declaration that Jesus had taught certain things would not be a mark of orthodoxy as distinct from heresy, and so that its inclusion would bear not at all upon the primary purpose of the Creed.

It should be remembered also that the Creed was far from being the only instrument used for the setting forth of the total Christian position. From at least the middle of the second century [4] the service included the reading of a selected portion of the Gospels; and regular attendance guaranteed a complete hearing of the Gospel materials within a comparatively short period of time. Nor can one read thoughtfully the other New Testament documents, and the writings of the Fathers, without recognizing that the ethical urgency of Jesus' teaching thoroughly permeated the mind and mood of the early Church.

Surely it is impertinent of us to suggest that the moral quality of Jesus' teaching was ignored by those who, like him, went to death rather than deny the faith; and the risk of death was a present and continuing reality for every believer in the first three Christian centuries.

Having said this, however, we must admit also that there was a definite theologizing tendency in the development of Christian thought. The first three Gospels represent Jesus as saying comparatively little about his own nature, and also as saying surprisingly little about the nature of God. In the Fourth Gospel the atmosphere is entirely changed. Here Jesus speaks a great deal of God, and of himself, and of their interrelationships, and of the relation of the believer to both. The Eastern Churches in particular continued to emphasize what we may call the Johannine mode of thinking; but the Western Church in its own less mystic and more literal way tended also to stress the non-visible aspects of the Christian pattern of thought.

It is easy to point out that such an emphasis belonged to the world in which Christianity arose. The contra-natural was preferred to the ordinary, the spectacular to the normal. Wonder tales circulated in every group, and the mystery cults competed one with another largely in asserting their respective triumphs over the common things of life. In a world whose Cybele had come down from heaven into Phrygia for the later saving of Rome,[5] and whose Isis redeemed Apuleius from the semblance of an ass,[6] it is not surprising that Christian propaganda moved outside the daily round of carpenters and fishermen and peasants. What actually is surprising, we should note in passing, is that in general the Christian wonders are intellectually as respectable as they are, and that Christian claims are characteristically much more largely moral than they are magical.[7]

The basic question, however, remains that of the reason for the development of any supra-natural factors at all within the specific frame of the Christian tradition. Granted that the Virgin Birth doctrine is in large part a declaration that Jesus had a truly human mother, why does it include also the assertion of a divine paternity? The answer to that we have seen in the impact that Jesus himself had made upon his followers, in Palestine and after: an impact that in the terms of that day required a special way of accounting for the phenomenon of his personality. The same applies to all the later declarations of the Creed about Jesus the Christ: his resurrection, his ascension, his place at the right hand of God, his second coming, his judgment of mankind. [8]

Things like this were not said of every man. That they were said of this one man indicates that there seemed to his followers to be sound reason for saying them. St. Clement's statement about the writing of the Fourth Gospel, as reported by Eusebius, may be applied equally to the formation of the Creed. 'Observing that the bodily things had been made known in the other Gospels,' St. John 'wrote a spiritual Gospel.' 'The bodily things' were found precisely in the tradition of Jesus' ministry, as rehearsed orally by the first apostles, as reported in the earlier Gospels, as repeated week after week in the Christian services.

But 'the bodily things' were in themselves so extraordinary that they seemed to demand some special explanation, some special setting in the framework of universal meaning. Therefore there came into being the 'spiritual Gospel' of St. John, arguing that this Galilean son of man must have been *par excellence* the Son of God. Similarly there came into being all those elements of Christian faith about the Lord which place him not in first-century Galilee but in the center of eternal values, and which are brought together in the Christian Creed.

So far as the historic teaching of Jesus is concerned, we may find its essence within the three Gospels called 'Synoptic.' Here the teacher speaks in Jewish terms, and of simple and immediate moral values. The sayings attributed to Jesus in the Fourth Gospel not only are alien to the Palestinian setting and to the thinking of those who heard him. They are also, if thought of as authentic utterances of the historic person, expressions of the most amazing personal arrogance. Not only is the human nature of Jesus absent from this Gospel; his human charm, his simplicity and his gentleness, are missing also.[9] But the problem disappears when once we realize that the claims here attributed to Jesus are properly not to be read in the first person singular, but in the third.

'He is the bread of life.' 'He is the way, the truth, and the life.' 'He is the good shepherd.' 'He is the door,' by which any man may enter into salvation. What we have here is the testimony of one who has found in Jesus Christ the true food of the spirit, the way into the knowledge of truth, the raising from moral death into that life which is eternal in its very nature. The Creed equally with the Fourth Gospel is a third-person document, declaring not what Jesus said about himself, but what later generations had found Jesus the Christ actually to mean and to be for them.

The 'back to Jesus' emphasis of a generation ago was a useful one, for it related Jesus anew to the daily problems of mankind. It was right in its assertion, but dangerous in its implied negation. Jesus indeed was a teacher, indeed was a heroic example, indeed was a beloved friend. But to infer from this that his life had no further meaning, that there had been no point in the effort to relate him to eternal significance and eternal value, was to make of Jesus the Christ a lesser figure than he had been for the Church in all the centuries, a lesser figure than he is and than he ought to be for all who seek to know him in fullness of truth.

The more modern scholarship doubts Jesus' interest in making supra-natural claims for himself,[10] the more must it take account of the force in him which drove others to make such claims on his behalf. That a Galilean peasant should be described as the eternal Son of God, without his having said so himself, appears a mightier witness to his character than any testimony of his own could be. The historically demonstrable details of Jesus' life are few; and for that very reason the historically guaranteed faith of the Church in him is the more striking and the more compelling.

We may say that the silence of the Creed about Jesus' ministry should not surprise us, in view alike of the general agreement on the Gospel tradition and of the contemporary emphasis on the supra-normal. What we have further to realize is that in truth this is not a silence at all: that it is rather an explicit declaration that the ministry of Jesus was of transcendent quality. That Jesus of Nazareth became for the Church 'Jesus Christ (God's) only Son our Lord' is precisely the summation of what Jesus of Nazareth had been to those who knew him, whether person to person in Galilee or by the transmission of the story and the experience in wider circles and in later time.

Thus the Creed is not in fact silent about Jesus as teacher and example. But for his example, but for his teaching, there would be no Creed, and there would be no Church to recite it. When we say the Creed, therefore, we are not forgetting the Galilean ministry. We are asserting it, not indeed in the bare bones of fact, but in the fullness of its revelation of eternal truth. 'I believe . . . in Jesus Christ. . . .' The historic Jesus here is fully present; and so also is the eternal Christ. To the understanding Christian the Creed speaks eloquently of both, and of both in one.

7. 'CRUCIFIED, DEAD, AND BURIED'

*'Suffered under Pontius Pilate, Was crucified, dead, and
buried.'*—The Apostles' Creed.
*'It was fitting that he, for whom and by whom all things
exist, in bringing many sons to glory, should make the
pioneer of their salvation perfect through suffering.'*
—Hebrews 2:10 (RSV).
*'They were in the way going up to Jerusalem; and Jesus
went before them: and they were amazed; and as they
followed, they were afraid.'*—St. Mark 10:32 (AV).
*'Do not listen, therefore, when anyone speaks to you apart
from Jesus Christ . . . who truly suffered under Pontius Pilate, truly was crucified, and died.'*—St. Ignatius, about A.D. 115.[1]

That the suffering and death of Jesus are crucial in the Christian Gospel every orthodox theologian would assert, and few
laymen would think to deny. Yet it is a curious thing that, in
most Churches, very little direct attention is given to this major
element in the faith. Palm Sunday, with its story of the tri-
umphal entry into Jerusalem, naturally is treated as an occasion
for honoring the glorified Lord; and the supreme day of glory
and triumph comes just one week later, with the celebration of
Easter. In between, indeed, falls Holy Week. But it has been
only recently that any Protestants except the Episcopalians
have paid much attention to Holy Week; and even in Catholic
and Anglican usage the services of that week commonly are expressions of personal devotion rather than enquiries into the
meaning of the events they commemorate.

Actually, the death of Jesus today receives the most mention,
aside from the ceremonial phrases of the Holy Communion,
within those ultra-fundamentalist sects which many of us ignore as being on the outer fringe of normal Christianity. Here
indeed the emphasis is repeated and unmistakable, with its key-
note expressed in the text, 'Without the shedding of blood there

is no remission of sin.' Today it is only in these 'marginal' Churches that one hears with any frequency such hymns as 'There is a fountain filled with blood, drawn from Immanuel's veins,' and 'Are you washed in the blood of the Lamb?'

At this point it would seem that the revivalists are the nearer to the original and the historic Christian tradition. The death of Jesus was central in the thinking of St. Paul, and of the writer of the Epistle to the Hebrews, and of the author of what we know as the first Epistle of St. John. It was elaborately discussed by the theologians, ancient and mediæval. It was the focus of attention in the preaching of most of the early Protestant groups, notably of my own Methodist forebears. What has happened to change the emphasis, to leave our modern Christianity relatively so silent about this theme that used to be dominant in Christian teaching?

The accident of the Holy Week calendar provides part of the answer, but certainly not all of it. The real difficulty with us probably is that we have lived so easy and comfortable a life that we look on any suffering with peculiar horror, and on death as something that ought not to be discussed in polite society. We are so tender-stomached that we feel faint at the very mention of blood; and we have swung back to some of the ancient Greeks in greatly preferring the poetry of Jesus' infancy, and the soaring imagination of his resurrection, to the brutal reality of his crucifixion.

This reaction may be in part quite healthy. When its motive, conscious or subconscious, is to repudiate the logic-chopping that was done about the atonement in mediæval theology, it brings us into freer and fresher air. When it becomes literate enough to observe that 'without the shedding of blood there is no remission of sin' is in its context not at all a statement of Christian faith, but precisely a description of that Jewish usage which the Christian faith is destined to supersede, it is returning to recognition of what the writer actually meant.[2]

We can afford to set aside, without argument here, those

elaborated theories of the atonement (my Professor of Systematic Theology made us memorize a list of seventeen different ones) which urged that Jesus' death was a ransom God had to pay to the devil, or a satisfaction of absolute divine justice, or a substitution of the innocent for the guilty. The only devil whose existence we are sure of is in ourselves; and we do not conceive of divine justice as being so unjust that it is satisfied when the guilty escape because the innocent has been punished. It is not in theories of atonement, but in the facts of experience, that we shall look for the meaning to us of the declaration that Jesus 'Suffered under Pontius Pilate, Was crucified, dead, and buried.'

Two periods of history concern us. I propose to take them in reverse order: first, the period in which the Church was defining its views; and second, the period in which Jesus himself lived and died. In more than one preceding chapter we have had occasion to notice those early heretics who held that Jesus could not have lived a truly human life. Just as they were eager to deny his actual heritage from a human mother, so they rejected the thought that he could actually have suffered pain, actually have died a physical death.

As in the case of the Virgin Birth, again, many who were counted orthodox Christians went far in this anti-natural direction. The Christian Platonists of Alexandria, St. Clement and Origen, of course were disposed by their general philosophical assumptions to deny the importance of physical phenomena. In the case of Jesus they went to extremes, declaring that he had required no food,[3] that he was 'entirely free from human feelings,' [4] that he was 'wholly passionless (apathes, the root of our "apathetic"), beyond the reach of any movement of feeling, whether pleasure or suffering.' [5] The form of the 'Nicene Creed' actually adopted at the Council of Nicea in 325 represented a curious compromise between the two points of view. While it said explicitly that the Lord Jesus Christ 'was made flesh, was made man, (and) suffered,' it omitted all reference to his being 'crucified, dead, and buried.' [6]

More nearly true to the original tradition, with its firm grasp on the human reality of Jesus, was the simpler and less official statement of faith which became our Apostles' Creed. It is true that in its earlier form it seems to have left out the word 'dead'; but it insisted always on actual suffering, actual crucifixion, and actual burial. The sentence quoted from St. Ignatius of Smyrna, who wrote his letters soon after A.D. 110, marks this human emphasis at its sharpest: 'Jesus Christ, who truly was born . . . who ate and drank; who truly suffered under Pontius Pilate, truly was crucified, and died.' [7]

Up to this point it would seem that the main emphasis of the Church was less upon the meaning and value of Jesus' death, in theological or metaphysical terms, than it was upon the historic factuality of the event. It was thus primarily an expression of the conviction that Jesus had been genuinely human, that he had shared completely in all of human experience. While with its Platonic background the Epistle to the Hebrews goes further in suggesting ultimate implications, it is perfectly simple and explicit here: 'To make the pioneer of their salvation perfect through suffering.' That is to say, Jesus could not be for men the true pioneer of their salvation from sin, their true leader into a new way of life, save as himself he experienced all from which man seeks to be saved. Practically identical with this in meaning is the last sentence of the chapter, 'In that he himself hath suffered being tempted, he is able to succour them that are tempted.' [8]

Thus the first meaning of the death of Jesus is that it was an essential part of his human living: that just as all men are tempted, as all men suffer pain, as all men die, so he experienced temptation, so he endured agony, so he entered the grim gateway of death. As in the matter of regarding the Virgin Birth as a supposed guarantee of Jesus' having been sinless, so also here, any supernatural avoiding of human experience would make Jesus meaningless as leader, as example, and as hope. Only the sound impulse of the early Christians, which made them decisive in their certainty that Jesus had lived truly as a man, can preserve for us any significance in the life that he lived and in the death that he died.

But how did he die? Do the manner and the circumstances of his death have any meaning in themselves? Some years ago an eager young theological student of mine, wearied by his study of the elaborate doctrines that had been worked out to 'explain' the atonement, burst out to me, 'It wouldn't make any difference to me if Jesus had died of a bad cold.' I found myself unable to agree. I believe it makes a lot of difference. I believe it makes all the difference in the world.

Why did Jesus die? Why did Jesus choose to die?— Or did he so choose? I think it is clear that at the critical moment he did choose to die then, at the hands of his enemies, rather than to escape. Nor was it by any means an easy decision to make. The temptation in the desert, at the outset of his active work, had posed to him the choice between the popular way and the right way. That temptation continued throughout his ministry; and it reached its bitter climax only in the garden of Gethsemane, on that Thursday night before the first Good Friday.

One Thursday night, before a much later Good Friday, I stood in the dark in that same Gethsemane. Behind me rose the sharp slope of the Mount of Olives. Before me, bathed in moonlight which did not reach us on the western side of that easterly hill, lay the white buildings of the city of Jerusalem. I knew how far it was to the top of Olivet behind me, for I had paced it off a little while before. From Gethsemane to the summit, and over into the desolate and unpeopled gullies rushing down to the Jordan valley, was just ten minutes' rapid climb. As that Thursday evening I saw the torches coming out from the city gate, and dipping down into the valley of the Kidron, my mind went back to the Thursday night of nineteen centuries before.

Here was Jesus, with the moonlit city before him, and the impenetrable gloom of the olive grove at his back. He had done the best he could, for now almost three years of patient, quiet teaching. What had he achieved? He had gained the hatred of the authorities. He had been alternately hailed and hooted by the crowds. He had been followed only by a few feeble, fumbling peasants. One of them, as well he knew, just the day before had sold him out. The others still were exhibiting petty selfishness over every issue that arose. Three of them, his three best friends among them all, had come with him but now from that upper room and that simple supper; and with the crisis upon them, they had no more imagination than to stretch out and drift off to sleep. What was it all worth?

Perhaps it was worth trying again, however. Perhaps he could accomplish more if only he could continue his work for a few more years. How easy it would be now, before Judas and the arresting officers came, while Peter and James and John still were asleep, quietly to disappear among the trees, quickly to scramble up to the summit—and over it, into the wilds where no one could find him, and where indeed no one would bother to follow. He could make his way down to one of the villages near Jericho, go into hiding for a while, ultimately appear again when things had quieted down.

Thus it was that he prayed, 'Lord, let this cup pass from me.' Thus it was that he wrestled with his problem, that he 'sweat as it were great drops of blood.' Morally it is not Calvary but Gethsemane, not Good Friday but Maundy Thursday, that marks the apex of Jesus' suffering, that carries the ultimate meaning of his sacrifice. Tempting as was the possibility of escape, it was temptation to the easy way, and the wrong one. To yield to terror now was to repudiate all he had taught, all he had lived for. If he ran away, none who had followed him ever would follow him again. The issue was before him: and only by facing it could he maintain his own moral integrity. Death lay ahead, and very soon? Yes; and Jesus liked the idea of death no more than do any of us. But now to escape the death of the body was to commit immediate suicide of the spirit; and, what was worse, to murder at the same time the spirits of all those who had trusted in him.

That passage in the writings of the second Isaiah which we know as Isaiah 53 was not written of Jesus. The 'suffering servant' of the Lord, in the prophet's thinking, was the nation of Judah. Her capital city destroyed, her independent kingdom liquidated, her leaders carried off into bondage abroad, Judah had lost everything she counted dear. And so: precisely so, only so: Judah had become qualified, said this seer of old, to lead the other peoples of mankind out of degradation and defeat and horror into that understanding of life which can make sorrow flee away and darkness be no more. This is the gospel of salvation through suffering; and it is the only gospel that offers true salvation to a suffering world.

The prophet's statement of it was not a prediction of the suffering of Jesus; and yet it was by a sound instinct that the Christian Church came to see in Jesus the fulfillment of what had been declared by the ancient prophet. The nation had fallen far short of living up to the prophet's dream for it; but this one man, undergoing spiritual torture far worse than the physical, choosing to pay the last full measure of devotion rather than to retreat from the values he had chosen: this one man had given living reality to what the prophet so long before had dreamed. 'The chastisement of our peace was upon him; and with his stripes we are healed.'

The reader may have wondered why I have included that little bit of St. Mark's Gospel, about the journey up to Jerusalem, among this chapter's texts. This seems to be one of the bits of personal reminiscence of St. Peter, preserved by his younger amanuensis. Here is that narrow, rocky, precipitous footpath leading from the Jericho plain up to the city set on a hill: perhaps a dozen or fifteen miles, climbing more than four thousand feet from a quarter of a mile below sea level to three-fifths of a mile above it. The whole party is making the climb; and most of them reluctantly, and with heavy hearts, because already Jesus has told them that thus to invade the stronghold of his enemies is to bring about his death. The whole party is climbing; but among them he who is to suffer the most, he who is to die, is not of those who lag behind. He is 'going before them,' he is leading the way. 'And they were amazed; and as they followed, they were afraid.'

St. Mark's Gospel seems to have been written in Rome, during those bleak and hopeless days just after St. Peter and St. Paul had followed their Lord in martyrdom. Again the Church was leaderless, again the cause was defeated. This little book, which in its earlier part moves so hastily that it covers more than a year of Jesus' ministry in a single chapter, suddenly slows its pace: slows it just at the point where Jesus first makes it plain that his death will be the inevitable outcome of his way of life. From that point on St. Mark treats the story in the greatest detail; and the detail on which he dwells is always that of Jesus' free choice to die.

What is the narrator saying to these Roman Christians? Just what he says in this snapshot from the weary climb up the mountains: that still Jesus is going before them. Are they amazed? Well may they be; but if they follow truly, they will not be afraid. Jesus himself is going before them. What then can they do, but follow?

Finally, it is the following that matters for us, as it did for them. The gospel of suffering may not be taken to mean that we shall not suffer because Jesus did suffer. If the pioneer of our salvation was made perfect through the things that he suffered, we may not ask to follow him by being ourselves carried to the skies on flowery beds of ease. 'Christ leads us through no darker rooms than he went through before'; [9] but if we accept him as our leader, it is through the dark rooms that we must follow if indeed we would be with him.

Long ago I heard a story of one of those revivalist groups which so often we hold in contempt; and when first I heard it I scoffed. The tale is that of the young girl, coming down the saw-dust trail and kneeling briefly at the 'mourners' bench'; but rising very quickly, with her face aglow, and saying, 'Jesus has saved me.' But the old evangelist takes her by the shoulders and pushes her down again. 'No, honey, no,' he says; 'you ain't cried enough yet.'

I myself had to grow older and wiser, and to suffer many things, before I saw any sense in that evangelist's point of view: had to grow older and wiser by the very process of suffering many things. At last it began to come clear to me: 'You ain't cried enough.' Is not that just what is wrong with our comfort-able life, and with our careless living? How can we know the meaning of life until we have plumbed its depths? How can we test our loyalties until they have been shaken in the storms of hatred and contempt? How can we call ourselves 'Christian,' until we know for ourselves something of the way of sacrifice by which Jesus became for us the Christ?

Jesus wept in Gethsemane; but he rose from his knees, and calmly he faced his captors. It is not for us to hope, in this chaotic and bewildering and devastating world, that we shall escape our meed of weeping. They who do not suffer in this world's suffering are passionless indeed; and passionless be-cause they are blind. But it is for us to determine that in this same world of chaos and bewilderment and devastation, we shall hold to our values: shall hold to them no matter what may happen to us.

'He truly suffered under Pontius Pilate, truly was crucified, and died.' Had he not, we never would have known whether he could endure the final test; and so we never could pledge to him our final faith. He suffered in Gethsemane, he suffered in the judgment hall, he suffered on the cross: and through it all he endured, through it all he kept the faith. Our suffering will not equal his; but in him is our hope that through what pain may be ours, the faith still shall be ours too.

'I have been crucified with Christ,' cried St. Paul; 'nevertheless I live.' [10] We are permitted to challenge the connective. Surely what St. Paul meant, what finally the Gospel declares, is this: 'We have been crucified with Christ; *therefore* we live.' 'The blood of Jesus Christ cleanseth us from every sin.' Rather than deny the conviction of his spirit, he poured out the blood of his heart. He who was truly human flesh did this; and because he did this we humans call him 'Lord.'

'Crucified, dead, and buried': and for this reason alive forever more. The way to life is through the valley of the shadow of death. Jesus himself is going before us, and still we are amazed; but if we follow him truly, we shall not be afraid.

8. 'HE DESCENDED INTO HELL'

'He descended into hell.'—The Apostles' Creed.

'Christ . . . being put to death in the flesh, but quickened by the Spirit: by which also he went and preached unto the spirits in prison.'—I Peter 3:18f (AV).

'Though Christ is God, because he was man also, he died according to the scriptures, and in accordance with the same was buried. With this same law he complied by remaining in the form of a dead man in the underworld; nor did he ascend into the heights of the heavens, until he had descended into the inner parts of the earth, so that there he might make the patriarchs and prophets sharers of himself.'—Tertullian, about A.D. 210.[1]

'The divine nature descended into death by the flesh, not that under the law of mortals it should be held by death, but that being raised by itself it should open the doors of death.'—Rufinus of Aquileia, about A.D. 400.[2]

'For instance, what sense can you possibly make out of "He descended into hell"?' Thus a young cleric who knew I was working on this book, and who heartily disapproved the enterprise. His question was a fair one; but as I ventured to tell him, I think it permits a fair answer.

The answer stands in terms of historic Christian thinking, and it is twofold: first, that the doctrine of the 'descent into hell' reflects a decent concern that those who lived before the days of the Christian Gospel nevertheless should have a fair chance at salvation; and, second, that the concept of Jesus the Christ as being subjected to the full experience of the human dead is yet another way of insisting that both his human nature and his human suffering were real. To this latter we may add a reinterpretation or expansion of our own, in the matter of what descent into hell may mean in moral and psychological terms. The

present chapter is an effort to implement the reply thus out-
lined.

My friend certainly had selected, for his challenge, what to
the modern mind is the most difficult single statement in the
Creed, and the one which seems the least readily to yield significant meaning. We have seen above, in the chapter which treats
of the history of the Creed in the Churches, that this clause has
been the most frequently omitted, and that when retained it has
led often to the supplying of explanatory footnotes. Nor is it included in Marcellus' text of the Old Roman Symbol, in the middle of the fourth century, though by the time of Rufinus it does
seem to have attained credal status in Aquileia if not in Rome.[3]
One might be tempted therefore to regard the concept of the
descent into hell as simply a late and unwarranted intrusion into
Christian doctrine, without historic authentication or moral
significance: which, quite clearly, is the way in which my inter-
locutor regarded it.

Yet the doctrine is much older than the late form of the Creed,
and from its earliest appearance it seems to reflect the two important considerations I have mentioned: that of the fullness of
Jesus' human experience, and that of the provision for the salvation of persons already dead. One of the presumed Scriptural
bases for the doctrine, the passage from I Peter quoted at the
head of this chapter, indeed is subject to challenge. Both Moffatt and Goodspeed adopt in their translations the guess made
by Schulz and Rendel Harris, to the effect that the original
reference here was not to the Christ, but to Enoch.[4]

It is true that in what may be the earliest parts of the pre-
Christian apocalypse called I Enoch, the protagonist does con-
verse with the imprisoned spirits, and transmits to the Lord of
heaven their petition for mercy (which, however, is not
granted.) [5] And whether or not the original text in I Peter read
'in which also Enoch,' it is at least possible that the legendary
visit of Enoch to the lower regions may have supplied the first
suggestion of the Christ's preaching there. But we are com-

pelled to recognize that the Petrine statement offers by no means the only New Testament hint of the doctrine of a descent into hell.

Thus, for example, St. Paul places the 'descent' and the ascension together in Romans 10:6f; though in this case he subordinates both to the living and realizable presence of the Christ in this world. More explicitly the Paulinist author of the letter to the Ephesians stresses the relationship of the two experiences:

> Now he that ascended, what is it but that he also descended into the lower parts of the earth? He that descended is the same also that ascended far above all the heavens.[6]

The natural implication in the account of St. Peter's sermon at Pentecost, that 'his soul was not left in hell,' [7] is that the soul is assumed to have gone thither for a time. Finally, as to New Testament thinking, I Peter 4:6 scarcely encourages the substitution of Enoch, even though the verb is impersonal:

> For this cause was the gospel preached also to them that are dead, that they might be judged according to men in the flesh, but live according to God in the spirit.

The early Church Fathers seem to have taken it for granted that provision had been made that the worthy dead of ancient time should have opportunity to hear the Gospel. Thus St. Ignatius says of the prophets, 'He whom rightly they awaited, being come, raised them from among the dead.' [8] St. Justin Martyr, and St. Irenaeus after him, quote as from Jeremiah (Irenaeus once says 'Isaiah') a reference to the Lord's descent to the 'dead people of Israel . . . to preach to them his own salvation'; and St. Justin charges that the Jews have deliberately removed this passage from the prophetic text.[9] St. Irenaeus makes it unmistakably clear that he regards 'the holy Lord' in his supposed quotation as being not 'the Lord God' of Israel, but rather the Christ himself, seen of course in the prophet's inspired prevision.[10]

Apocryphal Christian writings of the second century join in attesting the prevalence of the concept. In the 'Gospel of Peter,' which Montague Rhodes James dates at about the year 150, and so roughly contemporary with St. Justin, a voice comes out of the heavens asking, 'Hast thou preached unto them that sleep?'; and from the cross that follows the triumphant Lord comes the answer 'Yea.' [11] In the 'Shepherd' of Hermas, whose date may be as early as the first years of the second century, the preaching 'to those who were asleep' is assigned not to the Christ himself, but to 'these apostles and teachers who preached the name of the Son of God.' [12]

The third text at the head of this chapter, that from Tertullian's treatise *On the Soul,* not only is the clearest early Christian statement of our doctrine, but also is the first to make explicit in connection with it at once the concept of the Lord's truly human nature, and that of the opportunity for the salvation of the ancient servants of God. While Tertullian had withdrawn from the orthodox Church a few years before he wrote this particular work, he is not to be regarded as a heretic on such points as these. Indeed, he continued to revise and to intensify his attack upon Gnostic denials of the Christ's real humanity. We may assume, therefore, that what Tertullian here sets forth was already standard Christian teaching; and thus we find the complete statement of the doctrine, with both of the essential values definitely attached to it, as early as the first decade of the third century.

In a very different vein the apocryphal document known both as 'The Gospel of Nicodemus' and as 'The Acts of Pilate,' dating perhaps from the middle of the fourth century, provides a vivid, imaginative, and very detailed account of the descent into hell as at least one author conceived it.[13] The story begins with the sudden coming of 'a golden heat of the sun and a purple and royal light.' The light is hailed by Isaiah, Simeon, and St. John the Baptist in turn, each of them in phrases attributed to him in the Scriptures. Adam and David join in, while Satan and Hades (a striking combination of Jewish with Greek mythology) rather feebly protest. The Lord batters down the gates, makes the sign of the cross 'over Adam and over all his saints,' and leads a triumphant procession out to salvation. According to one copy of the text, 'The Lord set his cross in the midst of hell, which is the sign of victory; and it shall remain there for ever,' [14]

At this point we should note the nature of the 'hell' that actually is involved in early Christian thinking. It is not at all the place of fiery torment connoted by the word 'hell' in our later usage. The Hebrew *Sheol* and the Greek *Hades* were essentially alike. Each was conceived to be a shadowy realm of the dead, without clear distinction as to personal behavior while on earth, and so without either blessed reward or bitter suffering. Thus the question as to whether Jesus suffered the 'punishment of hell,' in addition to the death on the cross, did not arise in this period, though it was discussed at some length during the late middle ages. What concerned the early interpreters was their conviction that Jesus had entered into the experience of all men in death as in life; and, as we have seen, also that in that experience he had continued to fulfill his mission as the bringer of salvation.

The former of these emphases of course is a continuance of the Christian assault upon all those heresies which denied the truly human nature of the Lord.[15] As Tertullian insists, the descent into Hades is the mark of further compliance with 'this same law' which made real his death and burial. Thus the clause 'he descended into hell,' which in our time seems to be peculiarly contra-natural in its emphasis, if not actually superstitious, turns out in fact to be another denial of acute contra-naturalism in Christian thought. The Church contended that Jesus had lived as a man; and accordingly it went on to declare that as a man also he had died, and that as a man he had shared fully in all the experiences that accompany death.

Even more important as an indication of the moral emphasis

that actually is involved in this part of the Creed is the second aspect of doctrine attached to it, that of the preaching 'to the spirits that were in prison.' Here again the paraphernalia belong to another age than ours, and to an alien set of concepts. The mediæval visualization is well known in the innumerable Cathedral representations of 'The Harrowing of Hell.' (The principal literary source of these no doubt is the second part of the 'Acts of Pilate,' mentioned above.) Here the Christ is standing at the gates of hell, most commonly with his foot firmly planted upon a massive but broken door. At the side of the picture are grouped some surly demons, obviously annoyed but also obviously defeated. Other demons are squirming beneath the door itself. Meanwhile to the lifted banner of the cross there streams the procession of patriarchs and prophets, from Adam on down; receiving at last the salvation which was prepared for them from the foundation of the world, and for which so long they have had to wait.

Let us admit that Christian particularism had become unhappily rigid, in the notion that only through specific faith in the person of the Christ himself might salvation be attained. Yet within the very framework of this narrow concept the Church found a way to modify it: and so attested a fundamental fairness of mind which could not but triumph over mechanical and magical notions. Closely akin to this is the primitive usage which St. Paul mentions, and which he takes pains not to condemn, in his major letter to Corinth: that of baptism for the dead.[16] In both cases it is clear that Christian judgment could not bring itself finally to condemn those who had had no fair chance; and so that the descent of the Christ into hell became the assurance that all men, whatever their opportunities upon the earth, are in God's providence permitted to find the way to heaven.

No doubt we would phrase it quite differently. With our knowledge and appreciation of non-Christian traditions, and also with our realization of the power of cultural conditioning, we would say first that truth is no monopoly of any single religious system, and second that no man may reasonably be judged by canons that have not been within his reach. The difference is in the last analysis one of verbiage, and not of essence. What is sought in either case is the raising of all of human life to the highest level: that is, to the divine. In ancient thinking the Christ provides for this, as concerns the religiously unprivileged, by his descent into hell. In modern thinking hell is dismissed as unreal, and the vision of the triumphant Lord is possible for all men in a universal and expanding realization of the truth.

Well and good; but the question remains as to what mechanisms are available by which the truth may be seized upon and known. And here there arises yet another possible interpretation of our difficult clause: one which the ancient teachers never quite stated in this connection, yet which is not wholly alien to their thought. It hinges upon the question as to whether Jesus did actually descend into a hell of such a kind as we in our modern sophistication would admit to be real. My own answer to that question is categorically 'Yes.'

Though the burning hell of Zoroastrian thought, which was carried over into the late middle ages and thence into traditional Protestantism, scarcely was a factor in Biblical or early Christian teaching, its moral aspect is by no means absent from the basic Hebrew-Christian tradition. In the New Testament it is reflected in the term *Gehenna*, rendered 'hell' in the version of 1611 but left untranslated in most of the more recent English texts. While in late Jewish apocalyptic writings Gehenna had come to signify a place of eternal punishment for apostate Jews, or (sometimes) for all wicked persons, in its original force it referred simply to the 'city dump' of Jerusalem, in the valley of Hinnom to the southwestward of the city itself. Thus the primary connotation of Gehenna is not that of the fire in itself, but of the disposal of waste and useless matter: and so of the rejection of waste and useless humanity.

Did Jesus descend into this Gehenna, into this kind of hell? Surely he did; and surely has Christian doctrine always realized this. What else is the meaning of Jesus' experience on the slopes of another Jerusalem valley, that of the Kidron? When in Gethsemane Jesus, knowing that his betrayer was at hand and that his closest friends had fallen asleep, 'sweat as it were great drops of blood,' was it not the hellish thought of personal failure and uselessness that thus tormented him? There is for man no hell worse than the realization that he is of no use in the world, no use to God or man; and so the worst of all hells is the Gehenna of total personal failure.

By all external standards of judgment, this was where Jesus stood on that Thursday night. The mission patently had failed, and its decisive ending was at hand. All the labor and all the love had been for naught. The teaching had been misunderstood, the example remained unheeded. This was hell indeed; and in this valley of the shadow the Lord entered in truth into the final tragedy that human nature might know. Verily 'he descended into hell' while yet in the flesh; and so he drained the cup as beaten men through all the centuries have had to drink of it.

This surely is integral to the doctrine of the real human nature of Jesus the Christ; and alike in the ancient and in the modern frames of reference this is the final attesting of the significance of Jesus' human experience. Were it not for this his descent into the Gehenna of human failure, the Christ could not be for man the herald and promise of a raising to newness of life. The wheel comes full circle here, for this is also the living force of the 'harrowing of hell,' the proclaiming of salvation to those who have been imprisoned.

This chapter began with a somewhat negative reference to my friend who was negative about the clause in question. It has to end with my hearty thanks to him for provoking on my part a restudy of the whole issue. Henceforward I, for one, shall say this four-word sentence of the Creed with new assurance and conviction, in a new appreciation of the profound moral content that from the beginning has belonged to it.

'He descended into hell' turns out to be something wholly other than a clause whose difficulties need to be explained away. It presents itself rather as a succinct declaration of two of the most vital and most uplifting truths of the Christian gospel. It reminds us that there was no human experience whose depths our Lord did not plumb; and it proclaims that there is no human failure so abject as to be beyond the power of the salvation that is in Christ Jesus. 'The Lord set his cross in the midst of hell, which is the sign of victory.' 'He descended into hell'; and thereby both he and we are prepared to be raised again from the dead.

9. 'HE ROSE AGAIN'

'The third day he rose again from the dead.'—The Apostles' Creed.

'Last of all he was seen of me also. . . . Now is Christ risen from the dead, and become the firstfruits of them that slept. . . . Flesh and blood cannot inherit the kingdom of God.'—I Corinthians 15:8, 20, 50 (AV).

> *'Though dead, not dead;*
> *Not gone, though fled;*
> *Not lost, though vanished.*
> *In the great gospel and true creed,*
> *He is yet risen indeed;*
> *Christ is yet risen.'* [1]
> —Arthur Hugh Clough, A.D. 1849.

It is more than accidental that Easter Day is the one Sunday on which almost every American, who calls himself in any way Christian, goes to church. Beyond Christmas, even beyond Good Friday, Easter symbolizes the ultimate Christian conviction. The Easter message is that he who was born of a woman, he who died on Calvary, became the conqueror of death: in his own person first, and thereby for all mankind. Thus this clause of the Creed is one of the most crucial of all: and its understanding correspondingly becomes the more crucially important.

When, however, we enquire into the documentary evidence for the resurrection faith, we are beset at once by intricate literary, historical, and philosophical problems. The earliest of our four Gospels, that of St. Mark, provides very little by way of information. The authentic text of the book ends abruptly in the middle of the sixteenth chapter. Here the women have found the stone rolled away from the door of the tomb. They are told that Jesus is risen and gone before them into Galilee. Presumably they see 'the place where they laid him.' Then they flee, 'for they were afraid.'

The remainder of the final chapter of the Gospel, in its familiar form, does not appear in the earliest and best Greek manuscripts.[2] On examination it shows itself clearly to be dependent on the other Gospels, summarizing briefly what is recorded at length not only in St. Matthew and St. Luke, but also in the still later St. John. An alternative and shorter ending, probably a variant attempt to provide a satisfactory conclusion to the incomplete narrative, appears in a few relatively early manuscripts of the Greek text.[3]

St. Matthew's Gospel reports the appearance of Jesus to the women as they are leaving the tomb, and a later gathering by appointment on a mountain in Galilee. St. Luke tells of the two disciples meeting Jesus on the road to Emmaus, of an implied appearance to St. Peter, of 'the eleven' (with the two of the Emmaus road) seeing Jesus in Jerusalem, and finally of the ascension from the neighborhood of Bethany.[4] The fourth Gospel has Jesus appearing to St. Mary Magdalene in the garden, to the disciples in the city at intervals separated by a week, and (in the appended chapter 21) to seven of them beside the sea of Tiberias. There is thus very little resemblance in detail among these narratives, the only probable identity of circumstance being in the cases of the Jerusalem appearances reported by St. Luke and St. John.

Nor is it possible to determine with any assurance in just what sense our several authors understood these appearances of Jesus to have been 'physical.' Much stress seems to be laid upon the empty tomb, which means the absence of the body from it; and St. Matthew takes pains to dispute the notion that the dead body had been previously removed. According to St. Matthew, again, the disciples on meeting Jesus 'held him by the feet.' St. Luke quotes Jesus as saying categorically that he has 'flesh and bones,' and so is other than a spirit; and goes on to declare that 'he did eat before them.' In St. John the doubting St. Thomas is told to touch the Lord's hands and side, though it is not clearly said that he does so.

On the other hand, there are several factors in the narratives which would seem to argue against a full physical embodiment of the risen Lord. Except in St. Matthew the appearances strike one as being singularly abrupt, and in two cases Jesus passes through closed (and presumably locked) doors. Similarly at Emmaus he vanishes suddenly out of the two disciples' sight.[5] The reader will observe that these exceptions to normal physical law stand precisely in the two Gospels, those of St. Luke and St. John, which seem the most eagerly to assert the physical reality of the resurrection body.

Before we leave the Gospel evidence, we may profit by noting one set of incidental items which may throw some light upon the nature of our whole problem. According to St. Mark, the women found at the tomb 'a young man . . . clothed in a long white garment.' In St. Matthew it is an angel who speaks to the women. In St. Luke we have 'two men . . . in shining garments.' One scarcely is surprised to find the formula working itself out mathematically in St. John, where St. Mary Magdalene looks into the sepulchre and sees two angels.[6]

This particular process of accretion and conflation occurred over perhaps forty-five years, from the first Gospel about A.D. 65 to the fourth in the neighborhood of A.D. 110. But the Gospel of St. Mark itself stands some thirty-five years after the end of Jesus' ministry, after the events which it purports to relate. One reasonably may infer that the course of narrative development did not start with St. Mark, but rather that this sort of change had been occurring continuously from the beginning. One wishes, therefore, for evidence as to the form of Christian thought about the resurrection of the Lord before the tradition took its increasingly definite shape in the Gospels.

It happens that we do have such evidence: not indeed so early as we might wish, but almost fifteen years earlier than the writing of St. Mark's Gospel. Actually our first resurrection narrative stands not in the Gospels at all, but in the fifteenth chapter of I Corinthians. Here St. Paul is arguing the case for the 'resurrection,' apparently against some negative opinion which has been expressed in the Church at Corinth. He discusses both the resurrection of the Christ and that of the Christian believer: and he makes the one the basis and guarantee for the other. It follows that he must conceive the two 'resurrections' to be the same in kind and quality.

This identity is borne out by what he says of each; but what he says points definitely away from what we would call a 'physical resurrection' in either case. As to the hope of the believers, he is categorical in his sharp distinction between bodies terrestrial and celestial, between the 'natural body' and the 'spiritual body.' What a Pharisaic Jew would call a 'resurrection' persists in the time element, in St. Paul's teaching that the change will come 'in a moment . . . at the last trump.' But the change itself is alien to Pharisaism, for it involves a decisive rejection of the thought that the physical body as such will be reanimated. 'Flesh and blood cannot inherit the kingdom of God.' This surely is absolute witness against any physical resurrectionism, properly so called, in the apostle's mind.

Then what of 'flesh and blood' in the case of the risen Lord? 'With what body' did St. Paul think Jesus to have come? The apostle lists a number of resurrection appearances, some but not all of which can be equated with those reported in the varying Gospel traditions. Then he concludes the list with his own vision, presumably that on the road to Damascus. Surely not even the hardiest literalist will insist that it was the physical body of the historic Jesus which the bewildered traveler saw then. Yet St. Paul treats this vision of his own as being evidential in exactly the same way as were those to the earlier disciples. Obviously this argues that he thought of the experience of the others as being of the same kind which he had: the revelation of a living person, indeed, but by no necessity the presence of a physical body.

That St. Paul says nothing of the empty tomb may suggest

that at the time of his writing that particular element had not yet found its way into the tradition. If it had been current, and the apostle knew of it, his silence would seem to argue that he thought it at least unimportant, and more probably irrelevant to his non-physical concept of the resurrection body. In any case it is clear that his faith in the risen Lord was in no way dependent upon, nor significantly supported by, the material circumstances of sepulchre and stone.

Behind St. Paul's argument, into the earlier stages of Christian belief about the Lord's rising, we cannot go except by implication. What the existing records do suggest is that, from the middle of the first century to the beginning of the second, there was a gradual elaboration of detail and a considerable externalizing of the experience as reported. The least physical view presented to us is that of St. Paul, the most nearly material are those of the third and fourth Gospels. Even so, complete materiality is nowhere declared, and clear evidence against the normal physical limitations of 'flesh and blood' persists both in St. Luke's narrative and in St. John's.

The 'rationalistic' explanation, hinted at in St. Matthew's reference to stealing the body away by night, can be quickly set aside. As urged by some German scholars of a century ago, it argued that Jesus had not died but had been in a coma, and that he later revived and was indeed physically present with the disciples.[7] Such a view rests principally upon the factor of the empty tomb, which as we have seen is certainly a secondary consideration in meaning, and probably secondary also in time. This coma theory necessarily rejects the non-physical elements in the resurrection stories, including of course the ultimate ascension; and so it becomes wholly arbitrary in its choice of materials for credence.[8]

Again what we have principally to consider is not the external detail of narrative, but the inwardness of meaning. So far as narrative is concerned, the Bible contains several accounts of physical resuscitation of the dead much less confusing than are those in the case of Jesus: two widows' sons said to have been raised respectively by Elijah and Elisha, the daughter of Jairus, the son of a widow in Nain, Lazarus of Bethany, Tabitha-Dorcas in Joppa.[9] Yet no profound religious faith springs from their asserted reviving, no Easter is celebrated because they came to life again. It is not the account of a physical event, but the conviction of spiritual quality, that makes the resurrection of Jesus important. Examination of the record as a whole drives home the fact that it was this conviction of spiritual quality which gave rise to what in the course of time came to be phrased as an account of a physical event.

As will be seen in the chapter following, which discusses the ascension, the doctrine of an actual physical resurrection of Jesus leads to hopeless confusion as to what happened to the physical body afterwards. What is worse, however, is that it leads to much more serious confusion between values material and moral. 'Flesh and blood cannot inherit the kingdom of God.' A religious faith which seeks to root itself in the stone before the tomb will draw therefrom no true spiritual nourishment. It is only in life that life can find its meaning: and it was in the living personality of Jesus that the early Christians found their assurance of the ever-living Christ.

For those who knew him, he could never die. His moral imperatives were immortal, his gentleness triumphed over the brutality of the cross, his love lived on without reference to his body's death. He could not die: that certainty was at the beginning. Out of it came the assurance that still he lived. By the necessities of symbolic expression, and especially in the terms of first-century thinking, the faith took outward form in an increasingly objective way of expression.[10] But the outward never was the essential for the first believers, even though it may have been for them a useful way of statement. For us, to whom its usefulness is less clearly apparent than are its contradictions,

the outward well may be set aside as the irrelevancy which
it is.

One wonders whether there is a conscious symbolism in the
lament which the fourth Gospel ascribes to St. Mary Magdalene: 'They have taken away my Lord, and I know not where
they have laid him.' Mary of Magdala could not find him in
the tomb, and she never would find him in the far distances
to which she thought him gone. But when her eyes were opened,
she found him there in the garden close beside her. Too often
we have looked for the Lord in the tomb of quibbling about
physical details, too often we have lost him in the distant places
of fine-spun metaphysics. We are not likely to find him there;
but we may know him near and living when we learn to see him
in the gardens and the cities where we ourselves walk.

Jesus lives on in the deathlessness of his life, in so far as the
records make that life known to us. Much more vitally, the
Christ lives on in the perdurance of all moral and spiritual
value; and the living Christ we may know daily in our own
living. Not only on 'the third day,' [11] but every day, he is risen
again from the dead. He is risen whenever, wherever, right
and truth and graciousness are alive in men and women. He
lived on in St. Paul. He lived on in the glorious company of the
apostles, in the noble army of martyrs. He lives on still in the
holy Church throughout all the world: and he lives in direct
measure as that Church indeed is holy.

The resurrection faith thus begins in Galilee, and before the
crucifixion. It continues evermore, and everywhere that the
living qualities of the divine life make themselves known. 'Last
of all he was seen of me also.' St. Paul was not the last to see him,
for the vision is eternally real to all those who can see. We shall
not predicate Easter upon flesh and blood, upon tomb and stone
and angels. We may know Easter daily, and fully in our very
selves.

The conclusive evidence is not documentary, but vital. The

conviction is less of history than of continuing experience. 'Christ is risen! He is risen indeed!' That we may say, in knowledge and with understanding, when the Christ has come to fullness of life in us.

10. 'HE ASCENDED INTO HEAVEN'

'He ascended into heaven, And sitteth on the right hand of
God the Father Almighty.'—The Apostles' Creed.
'Ye men of Galilee, why stand ye gazing up into heaven?'
—Acts 1:11 (AV).
'Lo, I am with you alway, even unto the end of the world.'
—St. Matthew 28:20 (AV).
'Yet a little while, and the world seeth me no more; but ye
see me.'—St. John 14:19 (AV).

When I was a small boy, attending a Sunday School in China,
I worked out my own theory as to who wrote the book of Acts.
We had been reading through the New Testament (this was
long before the day of 'graded' Sunday School lessons), and
the week before had finished the Gospel of St. John. I had
noticed that St. John had no story of Jesus' ascension; and since
Acts began with that story, I quite naturally concluded that this
new and next succeeding book was a sequel by the same author.
A wise and helpful teacher straightened me out; but he had
sense enough to recognize that, on the basis of the data available
to me, I had made a fairly reasonable guess.

The curious thing is that the book of Acts actually comes
from the same hand as does the only one of the Gospels to carry
the ascension story. Whether we ascribe the two works in their
present form directly to St. Luke, or content ourselves with
saying that St. Paul's 'beloved physician' had a hand somewhere
in the course of their composition, we must recognize that the
two documents bear the unmistakable marks of a single authorship. The 'former treatise,' mentioned in the preface to
Theophilus which introduces the story of the apostolic Church,
clearly is St. Luke's Gospel, which also is addressed to this
reader Theophilus.[1]

The significance of all this for us is simply that for the detailed
story of Jesus' ascension we have the witness of one New Testa-

ment writer only. No one of the other Gospels alludes to the ascent from the mountain-top, nor does any other New Testament book make more than passing reference to the Lord's ascension.[2] The event is narrated briefly at the close of St. Luke's Gospel, as the final episode of Jesus' earthly ministry, and at greater length at the beginning of the Acts, as the opening of the history of the Christian Church. In the Gospel it is said that Jesus 'was parted from them, and carried up into heaven.' In the Acts the statement is that 'while they beheld, he was taken up; and a cloud received him out of their sight.' In general the two narratives are similar, though not slavishly identical. One speaks of Bethany, and the other of the Mount of Olives: a difference which is technically permissible, since Bethany is round the shoulder of Olivet in a southeasterly direction from the city of Jerusalem.

What gives us pause is the fact that no one of the other Gospel writers supplies any ascension story at all. This would seem to be a strange lack, in view of the wondering that naturally would arise as to what had become of the resurrected body of Jesus.— It is a strange lack indeed; and therein probably stands the reason for St. Luke's attempt to fill the gap. Of the three earlier Gospels, called 'Synoptic,' St. Luke's is the only one positively not written by a Palestinian, the only one whose traditional authorship is wholly apart from the circle of Jesus' personal acquaintance. What St. Mark's Gospel had as its original ending we do not know, and probably never shall; [3] as now it stands it breaks off with the women fleeing from the empty tomb, and tells us nothing of the resurrection of Jesus as such. St. Matthew's account ends not near Jerusalem at all, but on a mountain-top in Galilee; and not with an ascension, but with Jesus' words, 'Lo, I am with you alway.'

As was noted in the chapter which precedes this one, the resurrection narrative in St. Matthew's Gospel offers no detail as to the kind of body which Jesus is supposed to have had. St. Luke's Gospel, on the other hand, lays stress upon the physical nature of the resurrected body: 'A spirit hath not flesh and bones, as ye see me have.' This is not at all the kind of theory about Jesus' resurrection which we may ascribe to St. Paul. As we have seen, St. Paul listed his own vision of the risen Lord along with those of the earlier disciples, and so both in his case and in theirs must have been thinking of a spiritual rather than a bodily presence. But tradition had followed its familiar course of elaborating detail and intensifying the wonderful; and the successive Gospels show the concept of the resurrection becoming more and more material as time goes on. It is not surprising that the relatively late author we call St. Luke, who begins his Gospel with the Holy Ghost assuming the bodily form of a dove,[4] should end it by insisting on the bodily nature of the risen Lord.

Once he had done this, however, he had created a new dilemma for himself. If Jesus indeed had risen in his physical body, where did that physical body go afterwards? Clearly it was no longer present. In view of the standard Christian theory, it could not be thought that Jesus had died once more. An ascension into heaven seemed to offer the only solution to the problem; and so the story of an ascension was supplied.

It is of high importance to observe that the author of the fourth Gospel, who had all three of the earlier books before him and used them as he saw fit, made no attempt to reproduce this contribution to the Christian legend. 'According to St. John,' the physical aspects of the life of Jesus, while real, are not worthy of central consideration. The prime emphasis always is on spiritual value; and the ascension and the second coming both are disposed of in the fourteenth chapter, quite deliberately, by making the return of the Christ identical with the coming of the Holy Ghost.[5] 'Blessed are they that have not seen, and yet have believed,' is the end of the authentic text of this book; [6] and faith beyond fact is the central value all the way through.

Thus, in the matter of historical evidence, we find that only one writer tells us the story of Jesus' ascension; that the two earlier biographers do not raise the question at all; and that the one later Gospel author intentionally sets the physical ascension aside. He whom we call St. Luke thought he was solving a problem by saying that Jesus had ascended into heaven. For us this physical solution solves nothing at all, but rather creates a new series of difficulties.

Half a generation ago a Professor at Northwestern University circulated, to five hundred active ministers and to two hundred theological students, a questionnaire about their personal beliefs.[7] Two of the questions, neatly separated by others so that the connection would not be obvious, ran thus: (a) 'Do you believe that Heaven exists as an actual place or location?' and (b) 'Do you believe that Jesus was seen by his disciples and friends ascending into heaven?' To the former question only 57% of these clergy answered 'Yes'; that is to say, 43% of them had realized that there is no room for a physical heaven in a Copernican universe. But to the latter question, about the visible ascension, no less than 84% answered 'Yes'; which means that at least 27% of these seven hundred active and future leaders of Christian thought solemnly were asserting their belief that Jesus literally and visibly ascended into a place which, they said, did not literally and physically exist. One would like to believe that the clergy of today would average a somewhat higher I.Q.; but one suspects that the confusion which this questionnaire revealed has not wholly been dispelled from the minds of many sincere and not unintelligent Christians.

Both because of lack of credible evidence, and because the event, as alleged, makes no sense in the framework of our modern thinking, we have to reject the physical ascension of Jesus as we did his physical birth from a Virgin. With the physical ascension we necessarily reject also the physical resurrection in its commonly understood form; for otherwise the problem that led St. Luke to invent the ascension story would remain. If Jesus' body actually came from the tomb, what became of it later? If it died once more, then the resurrection loses all meaning. If it did not die, it either stayed on earth or it went elsewhere. Nowhere in the Christian tradition was it ever said that Jesus tarried physically among men longer than the 'forty days.' And there was no 'elsewhere' for his body to go, except to a physical heaven; which to the modern mind is plainly absurd.

So long as we think to predicate our Christian faith upon allegations about physical events, we are badly handicapped at two points. The less important of these is that we find ourselves quibbling endlessly about the historic evidence; and, as we have seen, the evidence for such supposed events as the Virgin Birth, the physical resurrection, and the physical ascension, is not of the sort that any qualified student of history could accept as even plausible, let alone convincing. The graver concern in all these cases is that we tragically confuse our issues when we seek to make spiritual values depend upon physical episodes. Moral and spiritual value are not thus to be found; and insistence upon the literal historicity of the incredible and the inconceivable is to no one a means of grace.

As with the other specifications in the credal paragraph about Jesus, so with the ascension, we must ask now, 'What moral value did this statement seek to represent?' We have seen that with St. Luke it scarcely was a moral value at all, but simply a way out of a dilemma which he himself had created by his materialistic understanding of the resurrection story. But by the time the ascension found its way into the Creed, it had taken on altogether a different coloring. No longer was it merely an escape from a narrative confusion. It had become rather the assertion of a timeless faith.

The clue is in the phrase which follows, and which has stood in that position at least since the days of Tertullian, late in the second century or early in the third: 'and sitteth at the right hand of (God) the Father (Almighty).' [8] The ascension now is seen not as the physical elevation of the body of Jesus into heaven, but rather as the spiritual elevation of the character of Jesus into oneness with God himself. So far as meaningful Christian faith is concerned, the statement of the ascension has the same intent and the same force as the describing of Jesus as 'the Christ,' as 'the Son of God,' as the divine *Logos* or 'Word.' No category lower than that of the divine seemed to the early Christians adequate to account for the life they had seen in Jesus; and they ascribed therefore to Jesus those glories which their tradition associated with the divine, including a throne in heaven.

A further difficulty that the literal form of the ascension narrative has caused, down through all the years, is that it connects directly with the idea of Jesus' physical second coming. The fourth Gospel, as we have noted, flatly rejects any such notion, saying that the spiritual presence of the Holy Ghost will provide the true coming of the Christ. In the following chapter we shall have occasion to consider the problem of the 'second coming' in greater detail. It is enough now to say that stress upon the second coming of the Christ, while supported by the actual phrasing of the Creeds, never has characterized the central teaching of the Christian Church. The reinterpretation made in the fourth Gospel, that of finding the living Christ in the divine presence in the human heart, always has been preferred; and has been preferred on the sufficient ground that it rings true in human experience.

Not believing that the body of Jesus literally ascended into a physical heaven, we cannot believe that it will literally return from that heaven. Rejecting both these literalisms, we are set free to apprehend the moral values that are involved, and that always have been involved. One of these is the recurring matter of the Christian estimate of the Christ; the other is that of our Christian experience in the Christ.

If we were developing the phrasing of Christian thought today, we probably would not think to describe Jesus either as 'the Messiah' or as the *Logos;* for one of these concepts is completely Jewish, the other definitely Greek. But knowing how Judaism sought for its national redeemer, how Stoicism held to faith in the divine principle suffusing all of life, we may use those Jewish and Greek categories significantly in so far as we have come to understand them. Whatever terms we use are in any event approximations only. The value within and beyond all the terms is that of the presence of God in human life. It is that of the Gospel of the incarnation. Having seen the character of God revealed in the Lord Jesus Christ, a man born of mankind, we are permitted to believe that the divine life may indeed become incarnate in ourselves.

Thus the value represented in definition, as to the nature of the Christ, merges with that which belongs to experience, in the presence of the Christ. As the physical ascension carried with it the idea of the physical second coming, so the full realization of the living Christ gives to us the transmuted second coming of the fourth Gospel: that is, the realization of the Holy Ghost in the hearts of men and women. 'Why stand ye looking up into heaven?' even St. Luke's supernatural visitors ask the wondering disciples on the mountain. Why indeed?

To look to the Christ may be to look into heaven itself, if we are willing to define heaven thus. And thus we may quite properly define it: for heaven is where God is, and so heaven is wherever we have found God in the Christ. But that heaven is not above the skies, it is not beyond our present reach. We have Wordsworth's authority for it that 'heaven lies about us in our infancy.' [9] Surely the poet knew more than that. Surely, when he thought more roundly, Wordsworth knew that the intimations of immortality are not limited to recollections of early childhood, that for the grown man they do not necessarily 'fade into the light of common day.' They are within our reach at any time: are within our reach whenever our own life takes unto itself the quality of the eternal.

In the calendar of the Church Whitsunday follows Ascension

Day by ten days. The values which these festivals symbolize
are not so far apart. St. Luke and St. John rightly belong together: St. Luke's account of the ascended Lord, and St. John's
faith in the indwelling Spirit. The Collect for the Sunday which
falls between the two major feasts thus makes the bridge between the Lord's ascension and the Spirit's coming:

O God, the King of glory, who hast exalted thine only Son Jesus
Christ with great triumph unto thy kingdom in heaven; We beseech
thee, leave us not comfortless; but send to us thine Holy Ghost to
comfort us.[10]

Most significantly then it goes on,

Exalt us unto the same place whither our Saviour Christ is gone
before.

How may we attain that place? But whither has the Savior
gone? He has led the way to fullness of life, and therefore he
has been raised to the place of highest honor in our hearts. How
may we be with him? Simply by following him: that is, by living
as he lived. Rightly to exalt him is truly to lift ourselves to heights
we had not known before; and so to be with him indeed. But
to be with him is to know the divine presence with us, and
thereby to know the indwelling of the Holy Ghost.

Once more it is value and not event, it is truth and not fact,
that gives meaning to our credal statement. 'He ascended into
heaven.' He did, for us, if he has been accorded the supreme
place in our own lives. 'Lo, I am with you alway.' That is true
too, if we will make it true. Perhaps after all St. Luke did well
for us in his creating of the ascension story; for we ourselves
can create and can renew the ascension of the Christ, if we are
willing to see him in all the moral grandeur that is his own. Nor
shall we cavil at those who have spoken of his second coming,
if only we have known the Christ coming to speak peace to
our spirits.

'He ascended into heaven.' We shall understand that, finally, when we have come to understand St. John's restatement: 'I will not leave you comfortless: I will come to you.' 'Yet a little while, and the world seeth me no more.' The world, alas, has seen him all too little. 'But ye see me.' We may, if we will.

11. 'FROM THENCE HE SHALL COME'

'From thence he shall come.'—The Apostles' Creed.

'As the lightning cometh out of the east, and shineth even unto the west; so shall also the coming of the Son of man be.'—St. Matthew 24:27 (AV).

'I will pray the Father, and he shall give you another Comforter, that he may abide with you for ever; even the Spirit of Truth. . . . I will not leave you comfortless: I will come to you. . . . Because I live, ye shall live also.'—St. John 14:16–19 (AV).

The enquiry into the doctrine of the second coming of the Christ must take us first into the background of Jewish thinking, many years before the time of Jesus. The strip of coastland and hills called Palestine, situated in the bend of the fertile crescent midway between the two great river civilizations of the Tigris-Euphrates and the Nile, inevitably became a scene of conflict between powers much greater than itself. Only for two centuries did the northern kingdom of Israel preserve its identity, only for three did the southern kingdom of Judah remain truly independent.[1] In turn the Egyptians, the Assyrians, the Babylonians, the Persians, the Greeks, and the Romans, overran the land and controlled the government.

In their bondage dreaming of freedom, the Jewish people longed for someone to deliver them from alien rule. The harsher and the bleaker their life, the more clearly the dream and the prayer took shape. Memories of the hero king David, surviving from the days of national freedom and national pride, suggested that surely the one to restore the ancient glory would be a member of the royal house of David. Kings in those days were not crowned, but in token of their kingship were anointed with holy oil; and so the Jews came to speak of the longed-for deliverer as 'the anointed one': in Hebrew *ha-mashiach*, 'the Messiah.'

The unknown prophet of the Babylonian exile, spoken of as the 'second Isaiah,' set aside the David aspect of the idea because he thought he saw the Messiah, the deliverer, in a foreign king: Cyrus of Persia, whose imminent conquest of Babylon seemed to promise new hope to the Jews.[2] Less than twenty years later the prophet Zechariah, campaigning for the rebuilding of the temple in Jerusalem, named as 'Messiah' the Jewish leader Zerubbabel, who indeed was a descendant of David.[3] Time, however, disappointed both the hope in the Persian and that in the Jew. Manifestly neither of these men could have been the true Messiah, for through neither of them had deliverance come.

Increasingly the failure of human effort pressed thought and hope into another realm. Not ever a majority view, probably, but an intense and influential one, was that which regarded the Messiah as someone more than human. The crucial passage in the Jewish scriptures is in the book of Daniel. Written during the Maccabean rebellion against Antiochus IV of Syria, about B.C. 165, it says:

I saw in the night visions, and, behold, one like the Son of man came with the clouds of heaven, and came to the Ancient of days, and they brought him near before him. And there was given him dominion, and glory, and a kingdom, that all people, nations, and languages, should serve him: his dominion is an everlasting dominion, which shall not pass away, and his kingdom that which shall not be destroyed.[4]

The new king is described as 'one like unto a Son of man'[5] in contrast with the four beasts which have been used to symbolize the earlier, non-Jewish empires of which the book speaks: the lion of the Babylonians, the bear of the Medes, the leopard of Persia, the fantastic monster that stands for Alexander the Great.[6] Compared with these, the Messiah holds the higher dignity of mankind; but, be it noted, he is by no means confined within ordinary human limitations.

What has all this to do with Jesus, with the teaching of the Christian Church about its Lord? We have to remember that Jesus and all his personal followers were Jews, trained in and taking for granted the categories of Jewish thought. Whether or not Jesus considered himself to be the expected Messiah is a disputed point. A generation ago liberal Christianity was practically persuaded that he did not, but more recently, especially under the influence of Albert Schweitzer, it has swung toward the opinion that he did. Whatever Jesus himself may have believed on this point, it is clear that shortly after his death: if not indeed before it: his Jewish adherents concluded that 'Messiah,' 'redeemer,' 'deliverer,' 'anointed of God,' provided the only category adequate to describe him. The burden of early Christian preaching, therefore, was that 'Jesus is the Messiah'; or, translating the word 'anointed' into Greek, that 'Jesus is the Christ.'

But it proved very difficult to establish the identification. Some Jews were thinking of the Messiah in terms of the book of Daniel, as a supernatural figure who was to come on the clouds of heaven. Others, more literally minded, expected him to be a military genius who would attack and eject the Roman occupation troops. The two groups were in complete agreement, however, upon the nature of the Messiah's objective: that is, that he was to destroy the foreign oppressor, to restore national freedom to the Jews. Had Jesus done that? Manifestly he had done nothing of the kind. Far from it, he had been put to death by Jewish demand and under Roman authority. How could he be called 'Messiah' at all?

There seemed to be only one way in which his followers could meet the challenge thus put. Believing profoundly that Jesus indeed was the Messiah, yet forced to admit that he had fulfilled no recognized Messianic function, the early Christians were driven to say simply, 'Well, not yet, but soon.' What Jesus had not done in his historic career he still would do. Returning from the sky in glorious majesty, as the Son of man pictured in the book of Daniel, he would claim the universal dominion and glory which are his by right. Thus, born out of the union of profound faith with bitter controversy, there arose in the early Church the doctrine of the 'second coming of the Christ.'

The chapter in St. Matthew's Gospel from which our first text is quoted is a direct expression of this Christian answer to natural Jewish scepticism. An earlier form of the argument appears in the thirteenth chapter of St. Mark's Gospel, which is known as the 'little apocalypse,' or 'little revelation.' The dependence on the book of Daniel is unmistakable: St. Matthew, indeed, specifically cites Daniel as authority.[7] Standing thus in the Gospels, which later Christianity came to regard as infallible statements of fact as well as of truth, the promise of a spectacular, supernatural, second advent of the Christ took its place inevitably as standard Christian teaching.

Such teaching from time to time has received great emphasis by special groups within the Church, especially in days of social confusion or calamity. In every century some have thought to read the future from the present, and in despair of this world to proclaim its immediate passing away. This type of teaching specially marks the revivalist groups of our own time, but it persists also in some local Churches within the 'standard' denominations. Recently there was a notable example in Southern California, when a minister set the exact hour for the Lord's return; only to admit when the time had passed that he would have to revise his calculations. He stands by no means alone. Over and over again such predictions have been made, and over and over again they have been disappointed.

In honesty we must note that the original expectation of the Christ's coming on the clouds of heaven was an immediate one. The Gospels are specific: 'This generation shall not pass, till all these things be fulfilled.' [8] That generation did pass, however, and so did fifty generations more; and these things have not been fulfilled in any visible way. The main stream of Christian thought turned away from literal fulfillment, seldom bothering to contradict but managing rather easily to ignore.[9] That, one suspects, is where the thinking of most of Christendom stands today. Few have given special attention to the doctrine of the second coming, and thus few have consciously rejected it; but few have allowed it to take a central or controlling place in their thought.

There may be encouragement in the fact that the same thing seems to have been happening even in the first century. In St. Matthew's Gospel itself stands a warning against those who are too sure in their expectation of time and place: 'If any man shall say unto you, Lo here is Christ, or there; believe it not.' [10] The trend is evident in St. Paul, and is fully clear with the author of the fourth Gospel. Not having known Jesus himself, and having taken over the body of Christian teaching as he had heard it (not altogether critically at first), St. Paul seems to have accepted the 'second coming' idea as a part of the authoritative tradition. Evidently he passed it on in his early missionary work, for in his first letter to Thessalonica we find him offering a rather labored explanation of some difficulties that have arisen about it. In a second letter to the same Church he pushes the whole matter off into a distant future; and never again, in those of his letters that have survived, does the apostle discuss the 'second coming' at all.

The fourth Gospel goes beyond ignoring to explicit and effective denial. Greek in the matrix of its thought, mature and reflective in its treatment, this new interpretation of Christianity turns attention wholly away from the material, phenomenal world to the realm of spirit and of ideas. It seems deliberately (as we have seen) to avoid any reference to Jesus' physical ascension, and thus affords no background for his physical return. More than that, it deliberately equates the Lord's return with the coming of the Holy Spirit. 'I will send you another comforter, even the Spirit of truth. . . . I will not leave you comfortless. I come unto you.' One remembers St. Paul's dictum in II Corinthians, 'The Lord is the spirit.' [11] When the divine spirit comes to man, then the Lord is here already.

What position are we, as Christians of the twentieth century, to take about this ancient doctrine and its varied interpretations? It is obvious that we must reject, frankly and flatly, any thought of a physical return of Jesus of Nazareth. To try to hold to it is to repudiate a Copernican universe, for there can be no physical return from heaven unless there is a physical heaven from which to come. In its literal form the whole doctrine belongs to that pre-scientific world view which we cannot for a moment accept.

We find ourselves, therefore, inescapably driven toward the position of St. Paul and of the fourth Gospel. 'Nevertheless I live: yet not I, but Christ liveth in me.' [12] 'I will not leave you comfortless; I come to you. Because I live, ye shall live also.' The second coming of the Christ is not an event in space-time, but an experience which transcends all physical categories. It belongs not to the sky, but to the human heart; not to the future, but to whatever present we are willing to assign to it.

We shall not appreciate fully the emphasis of the later Christian thinkers, however, unless we try sincerely to understand the thought processes of the earlier ones. They developed this doctrine, they got into this logical muddle and into what we consider this unscientific absurdity, because they began by saying that Jesus was the promised Messiah. What led them to say that in the first place?

Yet again the answer must stand in what they had found Jesus to be. A peasant of provincial Galilee, a friend of fishermen and of tax-collectors, he rose so far above their ordinary experience of humankind that the ordinary ways of classifying men simply were not adequate. They had met the wise men in the Synagogues, but he was wiser. They had known kindness, and had practised it; but he was more gentle, more gracious, less pretentious, than they had supposed anyone might be. They had dreamed dreams of a better world, wherein without hindrance men might live an ideal life; but in the same weary, bitter world of today he had shown that still the ideal life might be lived, for he himself had lived it.

The only description they could attach to him was the highest and the best in their vocabulary; and for a first-century Jew, that description could not be other than 'Messiah.' Surely none but the anointed of God could have such wisdom, could be so kind, could express so fully the best that is in man. He had failed to do the Messiah's work? That was true; and in their limited ways of thinking it had to follow that still he would. But their faith that he was indeed the Messiah never wavered. It did not waver because it was rooted so deeply in their knowledge of the life that he had lived.

In these terms the early Messianists are not so far from St. Paul and St. John; nor need we leave them far away from us. Here all types of Christian thought and teaching are at one, for all stem from the personality of that Jesus whom the Christians chose to call the Christ. With the great apostles the emphasis soon became a mystical one, urging the indwelling presence of the divine life in the life of man. The fourth Gospel deliberately uses its dual definition of that divine life, the Christ and the Holy Spirit. St. Paul is content with one form of expression here, in the living Christ. The difference between them is verbal. The unity is what is real.

For today, then, a valid doctrine of the second coming must be not physical, but spiritual; not future, but present; not one of the return of Jesus of Nazareth, but one of the indwelling of the Holy Ghost. Yet if the doctrine remain a doctrine only, it has no more genuine meaning for us than has the more childish view of the first believers. 'He shall come again.' This is a matter not of opinion, but of experience. We may read and discuss the documents never so carefully, analyze and criticize them to the last detail, and never know what really they are about. Indeed we should read the documents, and we should learn to discriminate intelligently among them. But we can and must do something more, something better.

Nor does that something depend necessarily upon full understanding of the intellectual problems. The writer of the 'little apocalypse' certainly was limited in understanding: but he was great in experience, and so great in his faith. He had found in Jesus the realization of all the best that he had dreamed, and more; and so he claimed for the Christ the fulfillment of all the highest hopes of his people. St. Paul too, without personal knowledge of Jesus, accepted the indwelling Christ as the power of his own life. Old and physically weary and very wise, the writer of the fourth Gospel found his comfort in the abiding presence of that ideal which Jesus symbolized and expressed.

In this realization we can go far beyond the announcement made by the minister in Southern California. We can predict the second coming, and accurately, whenever we will: whenever, that is, we commit ourselves to the ideal that for us is the Christ. To be true to the truest in life, the most beautiful, the best: that is to ensure the Christ's coming now. To continue true to beauty, truth, and goodness: that is to make the Christ forever alive in our midst, and in our hearts. 'If any man shall say unto you, Lo here is Christ, or there; believe it not.' We know where he is. He is in us, if we are willing to admit him. He is far away, and never shall return, if in us ugliness, and lies, and evil, crowd him out. The final doctrine of the second coming is that we determine its reality, each of us for himself.

If we make room for this quality of life, the light truly will shine from the east to the uttermost limits of the west. If we commit ourselves to this ideal, life in us is born anew. The 'second coming' paragraph in the fourth Gospel begins with a sentence which has not here been quoted, but which is crucial to the whole issue. 'If ye love me,' says Jesus at the last supper, 'keep my commandments.' To accept the way of the Christ, the ideal of the Christ: this is his second coming to man, and this is the indwelling presence of the Holy Ghost. 'He shall come again.' Not on the clouds of heaven, but in the hearts of men and women, shall the eternal Christ be known.

12. *'TO JUDGE THE QUICK AND THE DEAD'*

> *'From thence he shall come to judge the quick and the dead.'*—The Apostles' Creed.
> *'And as* (Paul) *reasoned of righteousness, temperance, and judgment to come, Felix trembled, and answered, Go thy way for this time; when I have a convenient season, I will call for thee.'*—Acts 24:25 (AV).
> *'As I hear, I judge: and my judgment is just; because I seek not mine own will, but the will of the Father which hath sent me.'*—St. John 5:30 (AV).
> *'The more and the better you know, the more severely shall you be judged.'*—St. Thomas à Kempis, about A.D. 1450.[1]

Always and in every way man is being measured, is being judged. Examinations are a judgment of the student, and of the teacher as well. Jobs are a testing of capacity and character, and so is life in a family. We are judged by others, we judge others, inescapably we judge ourselves. Both judging and being judged are for all of us continuous and inevitable. With what judgment then shall we judge? By what measure shall we be measured?

The historic Christian answer is that judgment is by the Christ; and it is the meaning of this judgment by the Christ that now we must consider. The particular symbolism reflected in the Creed belongs to the days when the Creed was being written. No doubt most of the early Christians took that symbolism as a matter of literal fact, though it may be argued that not all of them did so. For us the literal aspect is the difficult one: so difficult that for many it has succeeded in obscuring almost completely the ultimate moral value.

How did the symbolism of the 'last judgment' arise? Clearly the parable of the sheep and the goats, in the twenty-fifth chapter of St. Matthew's Gospel, is one point of departure. Though this section commonly is called a 'parable,' its phrasing is in a simple future tense; and it is not surprising that simple people should have thought that Jesus would indeed sit on a throne, at the end of human history, to pass judgment upon all men and women. A somewhat more difficult question to answer is how this concept, parable or not, found its way into the Gospel in the first place.

A generation ago, liberal Biblical scholars tended to say that anything attributed to Jesus which did not fit into modern philosophical thinking was not properly to be assigned to him: that we could believe he had said the things recorded in the Sermon on the Mount, which were matters of simple personal ethics; and also those things reported by St. Luke which reflect an acute social concern; but not the recorded statements about the end of the world and about the coming of the Son of man. A slight variant of that view was to the effect that Jesus did say these things indeed, but not about himself: that while he shared the Messianic hopes of his Jewish associates, he had no idea that he himself was to be identified as the Messiah.

Thanks chiefly to that extraordinary man Albert Schweitzer, theologian and lawyer and missionary doctor and Bach organist, scholarly opinion on these points has been largely reoriented.[2] Schweitzer went so far as to argue that what is called apocalyptic: that is, concern with the end of the world, with the judgment of the wicked and the triumph of the righteous: absolutely dominated all of Jesus' thinking, and controlled all that he taught. That, some of us hold, is an extreme view not supported by the total evidence. But we must admit that we have no right to wipe out Gospel materials as being unauthentic [3] just because we do not like them or do not agree with them. The fact with which we have to reckon here is that Jesus' reported sayings about the world future, in these supernatural terms, are in general as well attested as anything else that is quoted as having been said by him.

Where did the Gospel writers, where did Jesus, get such views as these? The answer necessarily is to be found in the culture which they had inherited: that is, in the thought of the

Jewish people during the last centuries before the Christian era. That God himself would judge the world was a natural enough expectation, as soon as God had come to be conceived in moral terms. In its earliest form, this idea was one of judgment and condemnation of Israel's national enemies, because of their opposition to the chosen people.[4] Soon, however, the ethically minded prophets began to insist that since God's judgment was necessarily just, it necessarily would condemn injustice in Israel and Judah just as decisively as it would punish wrongdoing in the alien Philistia or Moab.

Thus the prophet Amos, after listing the crimes and sins of all the neighboring peoples, swings upon the nation of Israel itself, and cries out:

For three transgressions of Judah, and for four, I will not turn away the punishment thereof; because they sold the righteous for silver, and the poor for a pair of shoes.[5]

Thus Isaiah, in the 'song of the vineyard,' declares that the Lord will destroy the unproductive vineyard of Judah:

For the vineyard of the Lord of hosts is the house of Israel, and the men of Judah his pleasant plant: and he looked for judgment, but beheld oppression; for righteousness, but behold a cry.[6]

Thus Zephaniah treated the Scythian invasion of 626 B.C. as a divine judgment upon Judah, because

Her princes within her are roaring lions; her judges are evening wolves. . . . Her prophets are light and treacherous persons: her priests have polluted the sanctuary, they have done violence to the law.[7]

It was well after the time of these prophets that the personal Messiah became a prominent figure in Jewish thinking. Indeed the majority of Jewish documents, even down to the time of Jesus himself, speak of what may be called a Messianic age, a time of deliverance and blessedness for the Jews, without referring at all to an individual person who should be 'the Messiah,' the 'anointed one' of God. It does happen, however, that a direct precedent for early Christian teaching about Jesus as judge of the world appears in the book known as I Enoch, written shortly before the middle of the first century B.C.

Here, after many sufferings on the part of the righteous, the Son of man will appear as the universal judge. All Israel will rise from the dead, and all men and women, as well as all angels, will face the final judgment. The fallen angels will be tortured in a fiery furnace, the kings and the mighty will be thrown into Gehenna, and other sinners will be annihilated. Heaven and earth will be wholly transformed, and the righteous will live in full happiness forevermore.[8]

We have noted several times that those Christians who had a Jewish background used the concept of the Messiah, of the divinely appointed redeemer, as the most suitable category in which to place that Jesus whom therefore they called 'the Christ.' It was inevitable that, having done this, they should assign to him the functions that the Messiah already held in Jewish thinking: and among these the most important and most spectacular functions that any Jewish document had mentioned. Thus, on the basis of documents such as I Enoch, the final judgment of mankind became an accepted corollary of the idea of the 'second coming' of the Christians' Lord.

We have seen also how at the beginning of the second century a thoughtful Christian, one who had been brought up within the Greek pattern, reinterpreted the whole matter. In the Johannine restatement of Christian faith in the Christ, the essential second coming of the Lord is found in the presence of the Holy Ghost in human experience; and so moral value takes complete precedence over physical event. It follows inevitably that this author should think of the judgment of Jesus as one not postponed to a single point in future time, but rather as immediate, continuous, and everlasting. 'As I hear, I judge: and my judgment is just.' The verbs in the Greek represent continuing action in the present; and since timelessness is of the essence of this Gospel's view, the judgment must be understood to continue on through the centuries and beyond them.

Since (whether we know it or not) our own philosophical background is essentially Greek, we shall find ourselves most completely at home with this way of treating the problem. To say that Jesus 'shall come to judge the quick and the dead' is to use the more naïve phrasing of Jewish apocalyptic. To understand in terms meaningful for ourselves, obviously we must think of that judgment which endures through all of life, and which recurs for every thought we think and for every deed we do.

What does it mean, then, to say that Jesus is the judge? We have observed that his formal assignment as judge of all men at the last day derives from the fact that the Jewish Christians had come to think of him as the Messiah. But why did they call him the Messiah? We have seen the answer to that too: not only in this series of enquiries, but whenever we have thought seriously about Jesus' life and character. People called Jesus the Messiah because he so far surpassed all other persons they had known that they felt he must be the supreme person of all; and so they gave to him the highest title of supremacy that they knew.

Ultimately, this means that Jesus is spoken of as the judge of all men because his life in itself measured up to and beyond the highest standards of human judgment. Messiahship, in the thinking of the first century, involved the responsibility of judgment. The personality of Jesus, in the view of all centuries, is in itself a judgment upon us all. To be judged by Jesus is simply to judge mankind by Jesus: that is, to judge mankind by those standards for which Jesus set the pattern. Inevitably we judge others thus. What matters more to us is that we shall be sure thus to judge ourselves.

Here some of the reported sayings of Jesus are much to the point, and will help us to find the way toward judging aright.

'Judge not, that ye be not judged,' he is quoted by St. Matthew; 'for with what judgment ye judge, ye shall be judged; and with what measure ye mete, it shall be measured to you again.' [9] That is to say, true judgment may not begin with censoriousness about others. No one whose life has been recorded for us was less censorious, no one was more understanding, than this Galilean teacher. And it is just because he, who was so rigid with himself, was so gentle with others, that his standard of judgment is for us impossible to escape.

The parable of the last judgment gives us more detail. The very fact that the setting was familiar to the hearers and readers made that setting secondary in their minds. The meaning and the application stood for them, as it should stand for us, in the particular basis of judgment that was set forth. Here specifically, as in his life and teaching as a whole, Jesus provides the testing and the measurement: namely that they who would be loyal to him, who would follow him, shall be concerned for every phase of the welfare of every man and woman. Set aside the spectacular paraphernalia of the judgment scene. Discard the literal throne, along with the literal sheep and goats. The truth remains, that the first and crucial sign of loyalty to him who came as one that serves is our own service to our human brothers and sisters.

The simplest expressions of Christian devotion always have caught this essential value, in which the final judgment of the Christ is critically determined by the personal example of Jesus. In the very first chapter of his 'Imitation of Christ,' before the sentence quoted as one of our texts, Thomas à Kempis makes the point:

He who would fully and wisely understand the words of Christ, must study to conform his whole life to the life of Christ.[10]

And in a more recent devotional classic, equally naïve and therefore equally compelling, the Quaker poet John Greenleaf Whittier pledges,

'O Lord and Master of us all,
Whate'er our name or sign,
We own thy sway, we hear thy call,
We test our lives by thine.' [11]

It is precisely in this simple but inescapable testing of our lives by the standard of the Christ that he becomes the eternal judge of all human living. We have found no better pattern, nor do we think to seek another. However careless, however callous, however brutal we may become, we still are brought back to the steadiness, the graciousness, the good will of the Galilean teacher. When we are dishonest, we remember in embarrassment the absolute honesty of his mind. When we are disloyal, we are challenged by the final loyalty of his behavior. When we allow ourselves to become cheap, we are reminded of how much his way of living cost him.

All this is true for all of us, whether we call ourselves Christians or not. It is true because down through the centuries the world has found no other way of judgment that so approves itself to our own deepest sense of moral value. Thus it is that the universal judgment of the Christ, not in a last day at the end of the world, but every day throughout the history of the world, applies to all men whether or not they consciously call him 'Lord.' 'All nations shall be gathered before him.' And all the nations are; and all that they have done must face all the while the moral scrutiny of his mind and spirit.

But there is special and particular judgment, as well as general. This is what Thomas à Kempis says in this chapter's final text: 'The more and the better you know, the more severely shall you be judged.' From that there is for us no escape, no way out. If we want to, we can play with the notion of escaping the moral responsibility that is upon us. I wrote the first draft of this chapter with the old mother cat sleeping on my big study chair, and her three plump, fuzzy kittens playing on the floor around it. Has the reader wanted to be a cat? Has he ever wanted a cat's freedom to do nothing, a cat's easy dropping off to sleep, a cat's facility for living in a pleasant house without paying the rent? The writer has: he has wanted those things often.

But as human beings, rather than cats, we cannot have them; and as intelligent and thoughtful human beings we may not even approximate them. The more we know, the better we understand, the more rigorously both the world will judge us, and we shall judge ourselves. Wishing that were not true will make not the slighest difference, not even in the matter of our own self-evaluation. No more than the Roman Felix can we put off judgment to a more convenient season. Intelligence and training force us to measure ourselves everlastingly by the best that we know or can dream; and so we who count ourselves well informed, we who pride ourselves on our ability to think, are called to the very forefront of those who must face the eternal, inescapable judging.

The world ever will judge us; and sometimes with less of understanding and kindness than really we deserve, for the world does not often take time to know enough about us as persons. More importantly far, we have to be the supreme judges for ourselves. By what judgment shall we judge? What will be our standard, our measure of what we ought to be?

'He shall come to judge the quick and the dead.' For us he has come already. For us he is here. Already and here is he judging every one of us. No one of us will face him quite unashamed, for all of us have fallen short of the mark. But since the judgment is a continuing one, the verdict too is ever subject to change; and so it is in our power to make tomorrow's verdict more favorable than today's. If we call ourselves Christian, we are challenged to 'conform our whole lives to the life of Christ.' If we do not call ourselves Christian, we have still to face the inner judgment of our own hearts: and so in truth to judge ourselves by whatever is the Christ, by whatever is the ultimate value, for us.

Ever will the world continue to judge both the living and the dead. It knows them all, it will judge us all, by the fruits that human lives produce. We assail ancient Roman tyranny, and recent German tyranny, and each new tyranny that appears among us. We condemn the traitor Benedict Arnold, and we condemn the traitor Quisling, and we condemn our own disloyalties. We repudiate cowardice and deceit in our fellows, and so ever we must scorn them in ourselves. Daily, hourly, we submit ourselves to judgment. Daily, hourly, we measure ourselves by the best that we have known. It is ours so to live that each day, no less than at the end of time, we shall face our judgment unafraid.

'My judgment is just, because I seek not mine own will.' Thus speaks the Christ of the fourth Gospel. 'Inasmuch as ye have done it unto one of the least of these,' says the Son of man in St. Matthew's judgment scene. Dare we be judged by the Son of man? Dare we judge ourselves by the Christ? Thus we shall be judged, and thus we shall judge. The Creed, declaring the judgment, demands of us the verdict.

13. 'THE HOLY GHOST'

'*I believe in the Holy Ghost.*'—The Apostles' Creed.
'*And the spirit of God was moving over the face of the waters.*'—Genesis 1:2 (GH).
'*Not by might, nor by power, but by my spirit, saith the Lord of hosts.*'—Zechariah 4:6 (AV).
'*Now the Lord is the Spirit; and where the Spirit of the Lord is, there is freedom.*'—II Corinthians 3:17 (RSV).

Many of us have been hazy in our concept of God, and confused in our thinking about Jesus the Christ. But the third Person of the Holy Trinity, the Holy Ghost, commonly has been hidden from us neither in fog nor in disorder, but rather in a perfect vacuum. We may have said that we believe; but many of us long ago gave up trying at all to understand.

Let us begin, then, with some people who are not at all embarrassed or uncertain about the Holy Ghost. They are the Portuguese Americans in the small agricultural towns of Northern California. The big fraternal order of this group, the lodge to which almost all the adults of Portuguese background belong, is the I.D.E.S.: *Independência do Espírito Santo*: or, as quite casually they anglicize it, the 'Holy Ghost Society.' The big event of the year for the California Portuguese is the 'Holy Ghost Festival.' This is celebrated on or about Whitsunday, the Biblical Day of Pentecost, seven weeks after Easter: about Whitsunday rather than always on it, so that the numerous local observances will not come all on the same day, and thus will permit folk to visit neighboring fiestas as well as to attend their own.

The traditional sequence begins with a big community party on Saturday night. On Sunday morning there is a parade, complete with brass bands, drill teams, drum majorettes, fireworks, and a 'Holy Ghost Queen.' After High Mass there is a tremendous barbecue, ostensibly for the poor and always including them; but including also everyone else who cares to come. Color and noise and gaiety and friendliness are triumphant; and in the name of the Holy Ghost everyone goes home very full, very tired, and very happy.

Our habit has been to look down upon, if not actively to resent, the color and noise of which the Portuguese are so fond. That is too bad. The California small-town Portuguese certainly are not great theologians. It may be doubted whether many of them could define the Holy Ghost in any articulate way. But they are real people, warmhearted and vital; and they have something to teach us in the very fact that they are so completely unembarrassed about the Holy Ghost. Indeed, their total lack of interest in trying to define 'the Holy Ghost' may suggest that they do know the meaning: and perhaps the Holy Ghost himself: at first hand.

Our own embarrassment in the matter probably arises first from the English expression 'Holy Ghost' itself. 'Ghosts' for us are associated not with Whitsunday but with Hallowe'en. They are night-wandering mysteries, constituted of white sheets or of ectoplasm (the choice here depending upon one's own metaphysical preferences), inhabiting full cemeteries and empty houses, speaking in hollow voices, or uttering unearthly screams, or dragging clanking chains. If ghosts are not evil, they are amusing. If they are not amusing they are evil. A 'Holy Ghost' scarcely can be evil, and does not sound amusing. The concept thus fails to fit into our normal scheme of things; and so the term 'Holy Ghost' has become for many of us words without content or specific reference.

Another sort of confusion arises from too literal an accepting of symbols used in the Biblical writings. The account in the book of Acts, of the coming of the Holy Ghost to the first Jerusalem Christians, has been badly mixed up with 'tongues of fire' and with the 'gift of tongues' as a supposed gift of linguistic powers.[1] The Gospel narrative of the Holy Ghost descending upon Jesus 'as a dove' [2] at the time of his baptism has led some naïve minds (as the late Professor Henry Lanz of Stanford University once put it [3]) to regard the Holy Ghost 'as a sort of mythological pigeon.' Fire, languages, birds, all are beside the point. All of us know that when we stop to think. It will be well for us then to think, in the hope that we may come to know.

In many Protestant circles in our own time the issue of the nature and identity of the Holy Ghost has been more or less avoided by substituting the word 'Spirit' in the Biblical and churchly texts, wherever the older forms read 'Ghost.' [4] This is not a happy way out. The use of a Latin word instead of a Saxon one always lessens the vigor of our English speech. The older English usage gives us 'Ghost,' a sturdier and more direct word than 'Spirit' is for us. By that older usage the present chapter will stand.

The discussion of words must be pursued further. Taking the chapter title and the quoted passages together, we have the key word before us in no less than four different languages. It was the (Hebrew) *ruach* of God that was moving over the face of the waters at the beginning of creation. It was the (Greek) *pneuma* which St. Paul [5] considered identical with God. It was the (Latin) *spiritus sanctus* which the old Roman form of the Creed asserted. It is the (Saxon) 'Holy Ghost' of which now we are thinking.

A colleague recently remarked, in this connection, that to his mind 'Ghost' seemed to connote something more nearly material than did 'Spirit.' That 'more nearly material' aspect really belonged to all of the words in their original force. *Ruach, pneuma,* and *spiritus* all meant strictly 'breath.' Since the breath was invisible, but early had come to be recognized as vital, and as the very token of continuing life, all the words (no doubt quite independently one of another, but for these identical reasons)— all the words, first denoting 'breath,' came to connote also the living quality of him who breathed. Thus God breathes into a clay figure, and Adam becomes a living soul. Thus 'a rushing mighty wind' blows down from Heaven, and the first Christians in Jerusalem find God newly present and newly powerful within themselves. Thus the divine spirit, the Holy Ghost, is breathed upon and into new apostles and ministers of the faith.

This mixture of material and immaterial aspects within one set of words is disturbing to the modern mind. There is something comical in the amazement of beginning students of the Greek language when they discover that 'pneumatic' may refer not only to tires but also to people: not only to tires that are air-filled, but also to people who are God-filled. We are uncomfortable about 'pneumatic' meaning 'spiritual' (etymologically the words are exactly parallel) because, being obsessed by late Greek dualism, we try to maintain an arbitrary distinction between the spiritual and the material; and because (under late Greek influence too) we tend to discount all that can be seen and touched and handled.

Some readers are going to judge that previous chapters have given definite support to such a preference for the unseen: in the insistence that believing is not seeing, in the making of the distinction between truth and fact, and in the stress upon the truth as being always the more important category. This does not demand, however, disinterest in the question of what shall be done with our lives in specific, visible, physical terms; and it may be that the present enquiry will help to redress the balance.

It is, indeed, precisely in the union of the seen with the unseen, of the intangible with the objective, that the Holy Ghost comes into the thought of man and enters actively into man's service. 'No man hath seen God at any time.' We have agreed to that, and so have most thoughtful minds since the world outgrew the fairytale mood of the earliest Genesis stories. Jesus of Nazareth men and women did see, though long ago; but the

Christ again is beyond the reach of our hands, outside the external vision of our physical eyes. God and the Christ are out of sight, and Jesus is ancient history.

Yet we need God, and we have him. We need the Christ, and we have him too. That always has been true, and is. And it is this present God, this God who is accessible, this God who is within the continuing process of the world, that the Church has come to call 'God the Holy Ghost.' God the Father was understood to be far away in Heaven. God the Son was believed to have gone away to Heaven years before. Nevertheless God was unmistakably here, and his presence could not be denied.

God was here in his children. God was here in courage and in devotion. God was here in faith and hope and love. God was here, in the unquestionable, undebatable experience of man. God, thus unchallengeably here, then needed name and definition. Hence the third Person of the Holy Trinity: *ruach elohim, to pneuma tou theou, spiritus sanctus,* the Holy Ghost: took his necessary place within the pattern of Christian thought.

Some years ago the devout and scholarly Bishop Charles Gore wrote three books on the three persons of the Trinity. The first two he entitled, respectively, *Belief in God* and *Belief in Christ.* For the third book he changed the formula, for he had to. He called it not *Belief in the Holy Ghost.* He dropped 'Belief,' and he added another factor: so that the title became *The Holy Spirit and the Church.*[6] One may regret that the Bishop thought it necessary to substitute 'Holy Spirit' for 'Holy Ghost'; but one may not doubt the significance of the other changes. The Holy Ghost is less in the realm of belief than in the area of immediate experience; and the experience of the Holy Ghost is available to men most readily in fellowship. The Holy Ghost is God in the life of man. God in the life of man is to be recognized most clearly when men come together in community of spirit and in comradeship of action: that is, when they come together in the Church.

We are not quite done with philology yet. To the Hebrew,

Greek, Latin, and Saxon-English terms we may well add the German (which of course is directly related to the Saxon): the word *Geist*. *Geist* indeed means 'Ghost.' But also it carries, in rather a special way, the overtone of quality. Thus the vividness and force of the compound *Zeitgeist*, which lamely and limply we render in English as 'spirit of the time.' Such Latinity robs the concept of all its vigor. The *Zeitgeist* is a force vital, strenuous, mighty: and the only legitimate translation into English is the literal one, 'Time-ghost.'

Der Zeitgeist, the Time-ghost, is the active, driving, determining force of the world in which at any given time man lives. It is impersonal and universal, but it is individual and specific too. *Der heilige Geist*, the Holy Ghost, is the active, driving, determining force of moral quality and moral experience and moral achievement. He too is universal and illimitable. He too is immediate and inescapable. He too is fully personal in his personal expression in our own lives.

And so, we come to see, we really have known and experienced the Holy Ghost all along. We could not evade the Holy Ghost if we would. And when we identify the Holy Ghost intellectually as well as experientially, we are relieved of all embarrassment about the term and about the reality alike.

There remain two questions of identity and relationship that must be looked at more closely. One is that of the relationship of the Holy Ghost to God the Father. The other is that of the relationship between the Holy Ghost and God the Son. These questions belong to historical theology rather than directly to personal religion; but it was from personal religious experience that they found their way into theological statement; and their clearing up may contribute toward a personal religion less disturbed by problems of phrasing.

The Holy Ghost as the spirit of God is self-explanatory. The distinction made between God and his spirit belongs first to the later and more sophisticated days of Jewish thinking, when God no longer was thought of as coming to man in bodily form. The earlier creation story, that preserved in Genesis 2, has Jahveh [7] doing the work literally with his own hands. The later one (some five hundred years later [8]), in Genesis 1, assigns the activity to God's spirit. It is God's spirit again, according to Zechariah, that is to energize Zerubbabel for his task of national reconstruction. It is God as spirit only whom the writer of the fourth Gospel holds we are to worship; [9] and this Greek Christian goes on to say that we not only are to worship God as spirit, but also must worship *in* the spirit. In these terms 'the Holy Ghost' is, simply, a designation for the present and accessible God.

Just how Jesus is to be related to the pattern it is more difficult to say. On this point Christian thinking developed and changed rapidly, and issued at last in one of the major controversies of Christian history. To begin with, the Gospels all report that the Holy Ghost came upon Jesus at the outset of his ministry, when he aligned himself with the mission of St. John the Baptist at the ford of the Jordan River. This is the same idea of the Holy Ghost as appears in the later writings of the Old Testament: the presence and power of God available in the immediacy of human life. So long as the Church thought of Jesus as having been a man of extraordinary achievement, so long the spirit of God was believed to have come upon him and into him in special measure.

When, however, in Christian teaching Jesus himself became identified as the Christ, the unique Son of God, he and the Holy Ghost inevitably came to stand in a new mutual relationship. The writer of the fourth Gospel, as an intelligent Greek, was concerned to wipe out what he thought the crass superstition of the doctrine of a physical return of Jesus. Accordingly, as we have noted with reference to the problem of the 'second coming,' this Gospel author deliberately confused the coming of the Christ with that of the divine spirit, of the Holy Ghost 'the Comforter.' [10]

If the statements in St. John 14 sound confusing, it is because they are meant to be. On their face they are so contradictory that the contradictions must be deliberate. Jesus is going away, and the Spirit is coming. But Jesus also is coming, and never is going away. Jesus and the Spirit perform exactly the same services of comfort and instruction. Jesus and the Spirit alike are seen with the eyes of the understanding heart, and no other wise. Again we must note that what the Ephesian teacher is trying to say, to his Greek Christian readers, is that the effective presence of the Holy Ghost is all the second coming of the Christ we need or ought to want.

So deeply did the Church feel that the divine Spirit had been specially revealed in Jesus the Son of God, that it was not content to think of him only as a receiver and a transmitter of that Spirit. It went on to argue that the Christ, not less than God the Father, must be the Spirit's very source and origin. Dispute over this point, as to whether the Holy Ghost derived from the Father alone, or from the Father and the Son (*patre filioque*), constituted the great *filioque* controversy on which finally the Western and Eastern Churches split apart. It is fully in character, too, that the Western Church should have insisted on the special reference to the person of Jesus, while the East was content with the Spirit of God in his own right. The distinction may seem to us one without significant difference.[11] Nevertheless the debate is important as attesting once more the impact of Jesus the Christ upon the minds and hearts of men.

From history we come back thus to the present, from problems of theological formulation to the data of our own experience. Previously we have phrased it in terms of our finding the living God in all that is beautiful, and good, and true. We have spoken also of the eternal Christ as being immediate reality for us. Now we recognize both God and the Christ, *patrem filiumque*, in the Holy Ghost. We recognize the Holy Ghost as God in the life of man.

'The Lord is the Spirit,' wrote St. Paul to his materialistic and literally-minded friends in the seaport of Corinth; 'and where the Spirit of the Lord is, there is freedom.' Inevitably, inescapably, the Holy Ghost brings us back to the Whitsunday of the 'Holy Ghost Society.' Our Portuguese fellow-citizens are not intellectuals, and by our prevailing standards they are not aesthetes either. Nevertheless in their Holy Ghost Society, their Holy Ghost festivals, they have made their way into the very center of the truth.[12]

They are free in the Holy Ghost. They know their freedom in a present God who is real and gay and glad; a God who is real in their own gladness and gaiety; a God in whose presence they are not afraid to be themselves. For the Holy Ghost's sake they put on their brightest pinks. For the Holy Ghost's sake they blow furiously upon their trumpets. For the Holy Ghost's sake they barbecue the beef. For the Holy Ghost's sake they feed the poor, and feed their own healthy and hungry selves.

And at least one Nordic-American wishes that the Holy Ghost, that God in human life, were as real to us as he is for them.

14. 'THE HOLY CATHOLIC CHURCH'

'*I believe in . . . the holy Catholic Church; the Communion of Saints.*'—The Apostles' Creed.

'*Ye shall be to me a kingdom of priests, a holy nation.*'—Exodus 19:6 (AV).

'*Wherever the Bishop shall appear, there let the people also be; even as, wherever Christ Jesus is, there is the Catholic Church.*'—St. Ignatius, about A.D. 115.[1]

'*Where the Church is, there is the Spirit of God; and where the Spirit of God, there is the Church.*'—St. Irenaeus, about A.D. 180.[2]

'*There can be salvation for none except in the Church.*'—St. Cyprian, about A.D. 250.[3]

Casual conversation suggests that another of the more difficult and confusing of the declarations in the Creed is that to which now we come: the reference to 'the holy Catholic Church.' Some of those who in ordinary usage are described as 'Catholic': that is, those who hold to the tradition of Rome: are very much surprised to learn that Protestants too are accustomed to assert their belief in 'the holy Catholic Church.' At the same time many Protestants, even while making the assertion orally, are puzzled by the usage and are uncertain as to its meaning. We shall have to start, then, with yet another enquiry into the histories and the meanings of the words that we use.

The most difficult of the terms may as well be considered first. 'Catholic' means simply 'universal': no more and no less. It is our English form of the Greek *katholikos*, while our 'universal' is an equivalent English adaptation of the (late) Latin adjective *universalis*. Since the Latin language had no word of its own for 'Church' (though an approximation was in reach in *collegium*, which since it was not used for 'Church' became the root of our term 'college'[4]), Latin-speaking Christians quite naturally took over the Greek word *ekklesia*; and in that connection they adopted also the accompanying modifier, so that the Greek *ekklesia katholike* was written in Latin as *ecclesia catholica,* the Catholic Church.

For ten centuries 'the holy Catholic Church,' whether as words or as concept, occasioned no real difficulty. There was only one body of Christians recognized as Christian, whether in Greece, Italy, Gaul, or Britain. Then the Western and the Eastern Churches broke from each other. Since neither would surrender its claim to universality, each retained the word 'Catholic' a' a treasured possession. Five hundred years later, Western Protestantism split away from Rome. For the less informed of the Protestant separatists the word 'Catholic' then became charged with unfavorable feeling tone, and was consciously avoided. Fortunately (at least as one Protestant sees it) the Church in England never gave up its faith in a universal Christian fellowship, nor its own claim to be a representative of that fellowship. Therefore the wording of the 'Old Roman Symbol' was preserved without change in the Anglican version of the Creed; and through all the years the followers of the English tradition have continued to declare their faith in 'the holy Catholic Church.'

'Catholic,' then, means universal. Our further enquiry may be organized around two major and specific questions: First, what is 'the holy Catholic Church'? Second, who belongs to the holy Catholic Church?

Immediate light on the nature of the Church may be gained by glancing at the punctuation of the Creed itself. In the current American *Book of Common Prayer* [5] the text runs: 'I believe in the Holy Ghost: the holy Catholic Church; the Communion of Saints: the Resurrection . . . ' etc. The editors' usage is an unfamiliar one; and the Methodist Church has made matters clearer by changing colons to semicolons, and the semicolon to a comma. In either case the intention is clear: as an item of faith the holy Catholic Church is set off from the Holy

Ghost, but is directly joined to the Communion of Saints. That is to say, in the opinion of these editors, 'the Communion of Saints' is not a separate category in the list of beliefs. 'The Communion of Saints' stands rather in apposition to 'the holy Catholic Church,' and thus aids in its definition.

The words 'communion' and 'saints' themselves perhaps need to be defined. 'Communion' here does not refer at all to the sacrament of the Lord's Supper, even though that sacrament itself is one of the historic symbols of the larger meaning. 'Communion' means simply 'fellowship.' (It will be recognized immediately how the term did come to be attached especially to the sacrament, as the supreme external act of Christian fellowship.)

Nor are 'saints' limited to those who now appear in histories and encyclopedias with the letters 'St.' prefixed to their names. All of the early Christians were spoken of as *hagioi, sancti,* 'saints.' 'Saint' and 'holy' are equivalent terms, respectively in the Latin and the Saxon cultures.[6] 'Sainthood,' 'holiness,' implies first special selection, second a special quality of life. The Christian community was a fellowship specially self-selected from the pagan world, and it was a fellowship specially marked by its religious experience and by its ethical pattern. Thus 'the Communion of Saints' was, and is, 'the fellowship of Christian people': and 'the universal fellowship of Christian people' throughout the centuries may be for us the precise definition of 'the holy Catholic Church.'

Some early comments on the phrase suggest that it was understood to have particular reference to the continuance of the fellowship beyond the grave, and to the participation of those now living with the Church of the 'faithful departed.' It seems odd, however, that if this were the original intent, the expression should have been attached after 'the holy Catholic Church' and not in connection with 'the life everlasting.' Even with this interpretation, the sense of fellowship remains dominant. Thus a relatively early preacher tells his hearers:

The Communion of Saints: Though here the gifts of the Holy Ghost are variously distributed, yet in eternity there will be fellowship in all things; and whatever any of the saints may have less in himself, he yet may share by the virtue of another.[7]

Attention must be given also to the word 'Church.' *Ekklesia,* signifying literally 'called out,' is a Greek term much older than Christianity. It appears in Greek literature of the golden age of Athens as the name for the legislative assembly of the democratic city-state. It was used in numerous other connections which we would call secular rather than 'ecclesiastical.' In general it referred to any orderly assembly, continuing or temporary, brought together for a specific purpose. The New Testament indeed contains one example of the word's application to an assembly which was not even orderly. The author of the Book of Acts uses it for the rioting mob in the amphitheatre in Ephesus, screaming for the blood of St. Paul. 'The *ekklesia,*' he says, 'was in turmoil.' In this case we scarcely would be justified in translating, 'The Church was in turmoil.'[8]

The Greek Christian community, taking to itself the familiar designation of assembly, *ekklesia,* 'church,' did in time become a definite organization. In St. Paul's time this Christian assembly had a series of functionaries loosely designated as 'apostles, prophets, and teachers.'[9] The apostles were the leaders, more or less (but not absolutely) identified as those who had known the historic Jesus in person. The prophets were preachers, assumed to be specially inspired by the Holy Ghost; while the teachers were the informed, but perhaps not the particularly illumined, members of the Christian community.[10] Probably there was at first no formal election held for any of these positions. Rather there was acceptance of these several kinds of leadership by common consent.

(There is indeed in Acts 1:15–26 the account of the formal selection of St. Matthias to take the place among the 'twelve' which had been vacated by the defection of Judas; but the tale is obscure in itself, and it lacks support from any other early source. It is evident that St. Paul's apostleship, to take a more important case, rested wholly upon his own claim and upon the Christian consensus, without formal action of any group, local or general.)

A generation after St. Paul, in the 'pastoral epistles' which seem to have been expansions of his genuine notes to Timothy and Titus, we find in use the ecclesiastical terms with which we are familiar in our own usage: 'bishops,' 'presbyters,' and 'deacons,' [11] The bishop was the *episkopos,* literally the 'overseer': his title being one used in both classical and first-century Greek for the director or executive of any kind of enterprise. The 'presbyters' were literally the 'elders,' the older men; not until much later did they come to be called 'priests.' [12] The deacons were the 'servants,' taking care of the material and mundane aspects of the Church's life, such as the distribution of relief to the poor.[13]

Yet another generation, and the idea of a universal or 'Catholic' Church had begun to gain power throughout the hitherto scattered and largely autonomous Christian groups. As early as the year 115 we find St. Ignatius, in Western Asia, rather clearly associating the authority of the Catholic Church with the presence of the Bishop.[14] In about A.D. 180 St. Irenaeus, the Western Asiatic who had moved to Gaul, was arguing that Rome must direct the Church's life because of Rome's *potiorem principalitatem.*[15] That expression is one difficult to translate, and so still more difficult accurately to interpret.[16] To St. Irenaeus it may have meant either 'more powerful leadership' or 'more authoritative foundation.' In either case it referred very positively to the primacy of the Church in Rome; and it marks the earliest clear statement of the Roman claim to direct the affairs of the Church universal.[17]

By the middle of the next century, the third of our era, the universality of the Church had come to be understood as being exclusive as well as inclusive. 'There can be salvation for none,' said St. Cyprian in North Africa, 'except in the Church.' This excluded not only the false teachers now called heretics, but also anyone who had lapsed from institutional as well as personal loyalty, and anyone too who had failed specifically to identify himself with the organized Christian fellowship. Thus Christianity became a matter not only of faith and morals, but also of maintaining good standing in a particular organization.

Were the saints of those early days right at these points? Do we need the guidance of the Bishop? Must we accept the authority of Rome? Is it necessary to belong to the institution? To all these questions the modern mind answers 'No,' and on perfectly sound and defensible grounds of logic. Bishops are human, and anyone who has worked under their direction knows that they are fallible. Most of us would hold that Rome has not always been right. Many of us have known profound religious experience outside any building, and quite apart from any religious institution.

Nevertheless it may be argued that the institution does matter: and Rome and the Bishops too. Without them not only would there be no Christian Church for us now to discuss, but also there would be no surviving Christian tradition for us to share. Rome and the Bishops, and their successors and their concomitants and their moral equivalents, represent for us the continuity of tradition and the effectiveness of fellowship.

A clerical friend in a Southern California beach town tells this story: He was standing in front of his Church before the Sunday morning service, while down the street poured throngs of people: down the street toward the Church, and on past it to the pier and the amusement zone and the beach.

There came along a family of four: evidently father, mother, older boy, little girl. The little girl was attracted by the Church, and was very curious about what went on inside it. A rather long discussion and argument ended with the father saying, 'Oh, come on; we can sing hymns, and pray, and worship God, just as well on the beach as we can in church.'

'But, daddy,' the youngster protested, 'we won't, will we?'

—'We won't, will we?' Therein exactly lies the first necessity of fellowship: the first necessity of the Church, of the Church universal and truly Catholic. No matter what splendid things man could do quite alone, the fact is that commonly he doesn't do them alone. He needs the comfort, the support, the inspiration, that are available to him only when he acts as a member of a community. The religious community is the Church. Very few of us succeed in being effectively religious except through the Church, or through some reasonably exact facsimile of it.

The Church is necessary to us for guidance as well. The total experience of any group is much richer, and therefore finally much more significant, than can be the sole experience of any individual among its members. That total experience of the group is made available in continuing tradition and through institutional leadership. For his every interest and activity man has created the appropriate institution, precisely in order to conserve and to transmit the collected and selected values of collective experience. As collector, preserver, and transmitter of religious experience, the Church is integral to continuing and growing religious life.

A third kind of necessity for the Church's existence belongs to the specific nature of the Christian ideal: that is, to the Christian imperative of service to others. Assuredly we do not propose to limit our service to those whose names are registered on certain membership rolls. But by the very act of serving one another, we do create a community, a fellowship, and so a basis for and a stimulus to membership. He who truly serves mankind finds himself inevitably allied, not only to others who serve, but also to those who are being served. This unity in usefulness is itself a Church: a fellowship of those who have dedicated themselves to constructive, creative mutuality of living.

The Church, then, is both an organization and a principle. The 'Church visible,' as the old terminology described it, is the institution officially existing. It has definite constitutional patterns, standard procedures, accepted rules of eligibility. It holds property, makes decisions, performs action. The 'Church invisible' overlaps this visible Church, and offers to it the sanction of ultimate values. The invisible Church consists not necessarily in people who have inscribed their names on a register of membership, but inevitably in all people who are likeminded in pursuit of the Christian ideal. Being human, most of us positively need the Church visible for our own effective, practical living. Being seekers of those values which we call divine, we belong to the Church invisible in so far as we are genuine sharers in the common spiritual quest.

It is patent that we could not finish defining the Church without slipping over into the second of the two questions: 'Who are members of the holy Catholic Church?' Here we must return directly to the problem of catholicity, of universality.

The signal and tragic weakness of historic Protestant Christianity has been its tradition of separation, of divisiveness. Once having split from Rome, the Protestant groups multiplied by repeated fission. We all are aware of the amazing multiplicity of the Protestant sects, and of the unhappy results of Protestant sectarianism. Every division that involves conflict, every division that expresses itself in hatred or in contempt, is a denial of the holy Catholic Church: is a mutilation of what St. Paul described as 'the body of Christ.'

Both the parents and the seceders are to some extent to be blamed. When catholicism is insufficiently catholic to find room for a new idea, it must be challenged to show proof that it is right in thinking the new idea not only mistaken, but also destructive. When separatists are so gripped by a new idea that for its sake they leave the general fellowship, they must demonstrate that the single idea is worth so much as to overweigh all the values of the hitherto united community. Had orthodox and heretics alike pondered more carefully these questions of relative value, the orthodox would less hastily have excommunicated, and the heretics would less hastily have withdrawn.

Essential to the Christian concept of membership in the holy Catholic Church is the principle of voluntary decision. Who are members of the holy Catholic Church? The Hebrew-Christian tradition answers, 'Those who personally choose to be members.' No one is born a Christian. No one can by Christians be coerced into true Christianity. People may be pushed into the form: as by infant baptism, or by too early confirmation, or by pressure at a revival service; but that sort of thing makes no one Christian in meaning and in fact. Some people, as in the days of the rough and ready Frankish King Clovis, actually have been offered the simple choice between being baptized and having their throats cut. That did not make them Christian either; and the Clovis type of procedure probably is one of the specific reasons for the moral weakness and spiritual unreality of much that in Western European (and so in American) culture has been miscalled 'Christianity.'

Our true tradition is voluntary, and voluntary only. Judaism was freed to set this pattern of voluntarism just when it ceased to be a political structure and became a religious culture. Those who individually rejected the call to be 'a nation of priests, a holy people,' ceased individually to be Jews. Early Christianity grew up not in a single locality, nor in alliance with any particular cultural unit. Only those who personally wanted to follow Jesus, those who sought personally to share the Christ: only those who were willing to pay a considerable price in discomfort, and sometimes in suffering: only those who chose to be Christian were Christian, were members of the holy Catholic Church.

Catholicism and voluntarism remain the poles of our own field of choice and action. Because of the course of prior history, over which we have no control, no one of us today can belong to any 'Church visible' which is truly catholic, absolutely all-inclusive: because there is today no such universal Church formally organized. As things stand, each of us has to choose for himself from among a number of formally independent structures, with various rules, various standards, various ways of behaving, various property rights and interests.

Happily there are signs pointing toward a new catholicity even in this formal, official realm. The miscellaneous and once conflicting Protestant bodies are learning to work together. They are becoming daily less distinguishable the one from the other in their usages and teachings and standards. Therein, one may reasonably believe, all of them are moving nearer to the central tradition of historic Christianity: though each brings with it its own special and important gifts. Even more significantly, catholicity of spirit today is drawing together not only the adherents of Rome and those whose tradition denies Roman authority, but also with them the Jewish community which is the cultural ancestor of both. Thus, in a catholicity of spirit and conduct rising above the separatism of organizations, Roman Catholics and Jews and Protestants are uniting in new and effective action for human wellbeing.

The heart of catholicity, however, is apart from institutions formally organized. The holy Catholic Church finally is, and has to be, the Church invisible: is and has to be that truly universal fellowship of those who are like-minded, who are Catholic in the universal experience of the Holy Ghost, the Spirit of God in the lives of men.

Here the individual, voluntary decision is absolute and final. Institutionally we may choose to be Roman Catholic, or Protestant, or Jewish, or nothing: though if one recognizes that human institutions are valuable, he will disapprove of anyone's being institutionally nothing. Institutionally we may obey Bishops, or be guided by presbyters, or run our own enterprises as independent congregations. Institutionally we could be one, but doubtless we shall continue to be many.

Whatever we are institutionally, we must decide personally for or against the Church invisible and truly universal. Personally we can belong to the communion of the saints, the continuing and growing fellowship of the faithful, or we can stay outside it. Personally we can believe in the holy Catholic Church enough to share in its life, and to be nourished by its strength, and to contribute to its growth in service; or we can deny the holy Catholic Church, and remain individualist fragments, incoherent, disintegrated, and meaningless.

On the rock of personal faith the Church is founded. In the communion of the saints, the universal and perduring fellowship of Christian men and women, the Church consists. By the mechanisms of organization, and the activity of leadership, the Church is kept alive, effective, and growing: the Church invisible no less truly than the Church visible. In that unity of spirit which is the very presence of the Holy Ghost is the bond of true Catholic identity. Through the free choice of free persons the membership of the Church is determined: the membership of the Church universal and invisible, everlasting and finally real.

We may, if we will, believe in the holy Catholic Church. We may believe enough to claim our membership in it.

15. 'THE FORGIVENESS OF SINS'

> 'I believe in . . . the forgiveness of sins.'—The Apostles'
> Creed.
> 'If your sins be like scarlet, can they become white as
> snow?'—Isaiah 1:18 (ARG).
> 'Thou shalt call his name Jesus: for he shall save his people
> from their sins.'—St. Matthew 1:21 (AV).
> 'All have sinned, and come short of the glory of God.'—
> Romans 3:23.
> 'In as much as one abides in him, in so much one does not
> sin.'—St. Augustine, about A.D. 420.[1]

There is genuine merit in seeking to follow an outline which one did not himself devise. It forces him to face, and to try to deal with, questions which otherwise he would have passed by. Thus it is for many of us in the matter of the problem of sin. St. Paul was obsessed by a sense of sin; and, as has been noted, he came to think of Jesus the Christ chiefly as the redeemer of man from sin. The great Northampton divine, Jonathan Edwards, is most widely remembered (if not most accurately known) for his terrifying sermon called 'Sinners in the Hands of an Angry God.'[2] The fundamentalist Churches and the traveling evangelists still talk about sin a good deal. But 'we moderns' are disposed to think St. Paul, Jonathan Edwards, and the revivalists old-hat, and in their continual harping upon sin perhaps a little bit lower-class.

The Creed can teach us better, if we will give heed; and life itself will teach us better, if we are willing to learn. We may begin by following the procedure used in others of these enquiries, turning first to the question of the meanings of words as they are used in the original sources. What is sin? What did the Biblical authors, what did the writers of the Creed, understand sin to be? Having understood their thought, as best we may, we shall be ready to ask how, and how far, it is relevant to our own experience and our own needs.

The key word, and that which stands in the early Greek text of the Creed, is *hamartia*, which means literally 'missing the mark.' There are several other and cognate words used in the New Testament: *parabasis*, usually rendered by 'trespass' or 'transgression,' and suggesting the overstepping of a boundary; *akatharsia*, 'uncleanness,' 'dirtiness'; *adikia*, 'unrighteousness,' or, more exactly, 'injustice'; and *kakourgia*, whose English equivalent is our term 'guilt.'

All of these are relevant to the Christian view of the problem: Christian whether in the first century or in the twentieth. And all of them are relevant to human weakness at any time in history. Aiming at the best, we fall short of it: that is *hamartia*. Knowing the proper limits of action or intention, we venture beyond them: that is *parabasis*. Given a clean page on which to write, we smear and befoul it: that is *akatharsia*. Accepting a standard of fair dealing, we deal otherwise with our fellows: that is *adikia*. And so, conscious of our shortcomings and our transgressions and our dirtiness and our unfairness, we are oppressed by a sense of guilt: that is *kakourgia*.

It would seem that recognition of these various sorts of human inadequacy is badly out of fashion today. To feel guilty is to be a neurotic, a psychopath, a schizoid, a paranoiac, or a manic-depressive. Justice is by some groups defined, explicitly and deliberately, as something conditioned by the economic class, or the national allegiance, or the skin color, of the person dealt with. Cleanliness has become a relative sort of thing, and so an uncertain one. And as for limits of behavior or targets for achievement, they were long ago blurred out in the pink fog of unconstrained and unexamined impulse.

These modern denials of sin and of guilt were natural enough as reactions against the contrary overstresses of an earlier day. One rightly may prefer the 'do-as-you-will' of the self-confident psychiatrist to the morbid and essentially fictitious self-searching and self-exposure that have been practised by some religious groups both ancient and modern. It is wholly probable that a wrongdoer who is quite unconscious of his fault is psychically more healthy, and is likely to be humanly more useful, than a rightdoer who tears himself apart over his own imaginary guiltiness. Both these people, however, are living in fictitious worlds. The Christian doctrine of sin is one that sets itself to deal with the real world of experience.

We may set aside, without serious argument, the notion that sin ever can be identified in terms of formal laws, or rules, or regulations. Crime can be, for crime by definition is disobedience to law. Sin is more subtle, and infinitely more serious. Sin is the violation not of what the external law demands, but of what our own concept of inner integrity requires. (Thus, for example, the only way some conscientious objectors during the war could avoid committing what they regarded as sin, was deliberately to commit the crime of disobedience to the draft law.) Sin is defined as disobedience not to the law of man, but to the will of God. Since, as we have seen, God is the best we know or can suppose, anything less than our own best becomes sin for us. Falling short of our best thus is precisely our *hamartia,* our 'missing of the mark.'

What unquestionably is the best story yet included in the Calvin Coolidge mythology is that about the Sunday when Mr. Coolidge had gone to Church while Mrs. Coolidge stayed at home. At luncheon Mrs. Coolidge enquired, 'Calvin, what was the sermon about this morning?'

'Sin.'

There followed a long pause. Then Mrs. Coolidge asked, 'Calvin, what did the minister say about sin?'

'He was against it.' [3]

That much is clear, and Mr. Coolidge stated it well and fully. By calling any kind of behavior 'sin,' by identifying any attitude of mind and heart as 'sinful,' we have taken sides against it. By recognizing it as sin we have declared our disapproval, our opposition. By so naming and so recognizing it we have pledged ourselves to attack it, if we can to wipe it out. We cannot take sin less seriously than that.

Perhaps the most serious confusion with reference to 'the forgiveness of sins' arises from failure to distinguish between sin and its consequence. Always there has been too much emphasis placed on the forgiveness of sins as providing escape from sin's results. This is, to begin with, a cheap way of coming at it: just as cheap as trying to 'fix' a traffic citation. It is moreover a way that by no means reaches the central issue of human sinfulness. Getting rid of sin's penalties is secondary. What really matters is getting rid of sin itself.

'Thou shalt call his name Jesus,' says the angel in St. Matthew's story, 'for he shall save his people from their sins.' [4] That phrasing is crucial. Jesus shall save the people 'from their sins': not necessarily 'from their punishments.' Psychology, biology, history, sociology, economics, unite to attest the closely calculable sequence of cause and effect, whereby wrongdoing draws unhappy consequences in its train. The patterns of habit, the adjustments of the synapses, the laws of human behavior (group and individual alike), the ratio of economic demand and supply: these bind in their mighty grip those who are lazy, or who overeat, or who tyrannize, or who enact 'protective' tariffs. What is done is done, and what follows after is thereby determined. Sin against the body, sin against society, sin against good sense: all should be punished, and are.

Is there then no hope? 'O wretched man that I am!' cries St. Paul; 'who shall deliver me from the body of this death?' His answer St. Paul found in the Christ as the savior from sin: again, let us note, the savior not from punishment, not from pain or purgatory or hell, all of which St. Paul himself knew and kept on knowing: but the savior from sin. To render the Latin Creed's *remissio* as 'forgiveness' in our ordinary English sense of 'All right, let's say no more about it'; or even to see it in the governmental terms of a judicial parole or an executive pardon: is to treat it far too lightly. *Remissio* is less than that sort of forgiveness, in that it does not promise our escaping what we have brought upon ourselves. *Remissio* also is much more than that sort of forgiveness, in that it does offer the hope of our escape from the power of sin itself.

Not the evading of hell, but the creating of heaven, is the promise and the power of salvation through the Christ. A tale anonymously inserted into the fourth Gospel,[5] but one not improbable in itself, tells us that the smug moralists of Jerusalem dragged before Jesus a woman who was a sinner. With that fine courtesy that was his, Jesus refrained even from looking at her. Quietly he said to the accusers, 'Let him that is sinless among you cast the first stone at her.' When they had shuffled away in due embarrassment and chagrin, he turned to her at last. 'No man to condemn you? . . . Neither do I. . . . Go and sin no more.' Did Jesus save that woman from sin?

Can we be saved from sin? We can. We can be saved by the same means, and in the same way. This is whither this enquiry has tended through all these pages: hither, to the salvation from sin that is the human outcome of all the Christian revelation. If by faith we find and know the God of beauty, truth, and goodness: can we then be other than beautiful, and true, and good? If by faith we recreate our new and more splendid Christ in our every new discovery in life: can we then live otherwhere than in our Christ? If by experience we know the Holy Ghost, the Spirit of God in the heart of man, can we walk otherwise than in that Spirit?

Manifestly this redemption is for us not often immediate, and certainly is not immediately absolute. Sin takes so little time, and its remission so long. The fourth Gospel's writer, in the little letter known as the First Epistle of St. John, treats of this matter by his familiar device of paradox:

If we say that we have no sin [he argues], we deceive ourselves, and the truth is not in us.[6]

Yet two chapters further on he declares:

> Whosoever abideth in him sinneth not: whosoever sinneth hath not seen him, neither known him.[7]

The clear mind of St. Augustine resolved the paradox. His comment appears in the last of the passages prefixed to this chapter: *In quantum in ipso manet, in tantum non peccat:* 'In as much as one abides in him, in so much one does not sin.' How Christian are we? Our lives provide the answer: the answer absolute, mathematical, inescapable. We are Christian in so far as we maintain in ourselves the high ideal which we have found in the Christ. We are Christian in so far as the Christ, dwelling in our hearts in the living presence of the Holy Ghost, drives out from us the evil that once held such sure possession there.

There is in the Latin form of the Creed a pun which scarcely can have been intended, since in that language it was inevitable;[8] but which none the less is rich in meaning. 'The forgiveness of sins' is, in Latin, *remissio peccatorum.* But if we ask how to write in Latin 'the forgiveness of sinners,' we shall find that we have to write that as *remissio peccatorum* too. In both cases we are dealing with genitive plurals. 'Sin' is *peccatum,* a neuter noun of the second declension; and so with the regular second declension termination for the genitive plural, *-orum,* it becomes *peccat-orum,* 'of sins.' 'Sinner' is *peccator,* a masculine noun of the third declension; which with the regular third declension suffix for the genitive plural, *-um,* also becomes *peccator-um,* but now meaning 'of sinners.' Thus when in Latin we say, *Credo in . . . remissionem peccatorum,* 'I believe in the forgiveness of sins,' we are saying equally and simultaneously, 'I believe in the forgiveness of sinners.'

At this point our ordinary English concept of 'forgiveness' becomes relevant indeed. Sin itself, once committed, is not forgotten nor wiped out. Nevertheless the sinner may be redeemed, may be so changed within himself that he shall 'go and sin no more.' Confused though the Gospel records are, as between the historic Jesus of Nazareth and the overlay of later theology, they are clear in attributing to Jesus the making of a sharp distinction just here. For sin the Jesus of the Gospels has no tolerance at all. He will not excuse it, condone it, compromise with it, for an instant. Yet for sinners he has all the tolerance in the world, all the tolerance of a limitless eternity. To turn to Jesus men and women had to leave their sins behind. Turning to Jesus, they found themselves in newness of life.

The forgiveness of sinners is what we sinners need: and what also, if we are to accept the Christ for ourselves, we shall practise toward other sinners like us. 'Forgive us our trespasses,' again and again we pray, 'as we forgive those who trespass against us.' [9] We are not so small nor so cheap that we shall expect, or ask, to have wiped out the natural results of our missing of the mark, of our overstepping of the bounds, of our dirtiness, of our unfairness. We are not so thoughtless that we shall hope to forget altogether the sense of guilt that has oppressed our spirits. In retrospect the game may not have been worth the candle; but the candle goes with the game, and we know the rules.

Yet in the strength of the Christ we are so strong, so daring, that we dare to ask and claim in him the changing of our spirits into the likeness of his spirit. In the purity of the Christ we are so clean that our minds and hearts no more offer lodgment to the befouling. In the justice of the Christ we are so just that we shall deal unfairly with no son of man.

Hereby we do know that we know him, if we keep his commandments. . . . He was manifested to take away our sins; and in him is no sin. Whosoever abideth in him sinneth not.[10]

'In him is no sin.' In him we believe in the forgiveness of sins, in the wiping out of the taint of sin from our lives. In him we believe also in the forgiveness of sinners, in the re-creating of ourselves into newness of living. His name is called Jesus, for he saves his people from their sins. They who will may become his people.

16. 'THE LIFE EVERLASTING'

*'I believe in . . . the Resurrection of the body: and the
Life everlasting.'*—The Apostles' Creed.
'If a man die, shall he live again?'—Job 14:14 (AV).
*'This decay must change to incorruption, this mortal to
immortal.'*—I Corinthians 15:53 (GH).
*'This is life eternal, that they might know thee the only
true God, and Jesus Christ whom thou hast sent.'*—
St. John 17:3 (AV).

Through a long and brutal decade death has pervaded our
world, and hammered at our spirits. Six years of war killed men
by the millions, women and children by the hundreds of
thousands. Daily yet, in lands across the seas, starvation and
disease add to the staggering toll. Scarcely one of us has not
lost at least an acquaintance, if not a friend or a loved one,
in the military service of the nation or in the chaos of the post-
war scene.

All this has had two contrary psychological effects on men
and women. On the one hand, some grew callous in despairing
self-defence: on the field of battle becoming quite casual about
corpses; at home reading statistics of numbers killed, and even
names, as names and numbers only rather than as matters of
human, personal concern. On the other hand, many of us developed a new and special interest in the destiny of those whom we
had known and loved, and whom physically we would have
among us no more. Men who entered the armed forces inevitably
calculated the mathematical chances of their own survival; and
just as inevitably wondered whether in any way they might
survive physical death in some new realm of personal experience.

It is of the highest importance, under conditions such as these,
that we shall learn to think clearly and specifically both about
death and about life. Luis Monguió of the faculty of Mills Col-

lege has pointed out, in a recent article,[1] that British and American people characteristically have shrunk from discussing death factually and frankly; and so that they have been especially lost and confused when death has come close to them and with spectacular violence. Such confusion we must become adult enough: in Mr. Monguió's terms European enough: to conquer. It is our obligation to consider thoughtfully all the data that are available, all the circumstances with which we have to deal.

The more gravely concerned we have been, the more perturbed, the more excited, the more carefully must we examine our ground, and the more rigidly must we adhere to reasonable reasoning. What we want, in any area, usually is different from what we have, from what we can have. In times of crisis the gap between desire and possibility is greatly, sometimes tragically, widened. Sanity in stress depends upon our knowing what we may hope to have, of what we want; and upon our proceeding then by those specific ways which offer some prospect of our getting it.

Within the Christian tradition the whole issue of life after death has been confused: confused seriously, and almost comically as well: from the very beginning. At funeral services the clergyman in the Church or chapel invariably assures us that the departed loved one now is with the Lord. Then, at the grave, he recites (or did until very recently) the ancient formula:

We . . . commit his body to the ground; earth to earth, ashes to ashes, dust to dust; looking for the general Resurrection in the last day, and the life of the world to come, through our Lord Jesus Christ, at whose second coming in glorious majesty to judge the world, the earth and the sea shall give up their dead.[2]

Recent revisions of ritual have softened this somewhat. The Methodist Church has relegated this form to an optional, and secondary, position in the Burial Service. The Presbyterian *Book of Common Worship* has eliminated 'in the last day,' and has changed the ending altogether. The American Episcopal *Book of Common Prayer* has substituted, for 'in the last day, and the life of the world to come,' simply the phrase 'unto eternal life.' But this revision is only partial; for in it 'the earth and the sea' are still to 'give up their dead.'

For almost all of us the confusion persists. We are accustomed to start with an assurance of continuing spiritual identity, unbroken by the accident of physical death. Then we shift abruptly to announcing a physical resurrection, at a distant point in future time. The contradiction is obvious to anyone who thinks; and for many of the thoughtful it has caused intellectual bewilderment to the point of weary dismissal of the whole matter. The wonder is that for so many centuries the Church and her leaders succeeded in avoiding so clear-cut an issue, in continuing to assert equal belief in both of these completely contradictory concepts.

It is not at all surprising, however, that both concepts did find their way into the early Christian tradition. The one, that of spiritual immortality, of the inevitable and continuing persistence of the real person, unconditioned now by a physical body, is a heritage from Greece and specifically from Plato. The other, that of the revitalizing of a physical body, came from Persia by way of the later Judaism of Palestine. Christianity, being both in personnel and in ideas a blend of Jewish and Greek elements, could not but have both theories introduced into her earliest attempts to formulate her own thinking.

Jewish thinking in the Old Testament is almost wholly negative as to any kind of personal life after death. Operating in terms of social wholes, the family immediately and the nation ultimately, Biblical Judaism thought of the future only as that of a continuing group and of a continuing tradition. When the writers of the book of Job posed the rhetorical question, 'If a man die, shall he live again?,' the answer which obviously they expected was a simple 'No.' [3] The author of Ecclesiastes says flatly that both men and animals 'go unto one place; all are of the dust, and all turn to dust again.' [4] Not until the book of Daniel, one of the latest writings in the Old Testament, does a clear statement of personal survival appear; and then it is one of a resurrection limited to some human beings rather than expected for all.[5]

The developments in Jewish thinking are well represented by three passages in the Old Testament Apocrypha. Ecclesiasticus, written in Palestine about 180 B.C., and so preceding the book of Daniel by some fifteen years, knows no immortality except that of memory and of surviving influence: thus its forty-fourth chapter, which is the basis for the catalogue of the heroes of faith in Hebrews 11.[6] In a section of the 'Ezra Apocalypse' which probably should be dated about A.D. 100, the day of judgment will see the earth 'give up those who are asleep in it, and the dust those who are silent in it.' [7] Meanwhile the Greek-influenced Wisdom of Solomon, voicing Jewish thought in Alexandria at almost exactly the time of Jesus, speaks quite positively of spiritual immortality altogether apart from the body.[8]

Let us rehearse the distinctions again: Original Judaism, and Judaism until the second century B.C., anticipated no personal future of any kind. The late Palestinian Jewish idea was that of physical resuscitation at a future point in time: that is what is called 'resurrection.' The Greek idea was one of spiritual survival, ever continuing, without beginning or end: this is what properly is spoken of as 'immortality.' The two concepts of life after death are wholly independent in their origins, and they are mutually exclusive in their meanings.

Our own confusion has arisen from the fact that primitive Christianity, having inherited these two incompatibles from its two major spiritual ancestors, tried to assimilate both of them into a single pattern of thought. As now will be obvious, both ideas made their way into the Creed. 'The resurrection of the body' is the Palestinian contribution: specifically the contribution of the sect of the Pharisees. 'The life everlasting' is the

Greek statement. And through the centuries the Church, having received this dual heritage, has tried to maintain a dual belief.

St. Paul may have helped to create the difficulty in his very attempt to clarify the issue. In I Corinthians 15 he argues for the 'resurrection,' and rings the changes upon the phrase 'risen from the dead.' Thus he would seem to be defending the Palestinian, Pharisaic point of view. Actually, however, what he contends for is not resurrection at all, but precisely immortality. The living Christ, he declares, has been seen by him no less than by the other apostles, and in the same way though at a much later time. Since St. Paul's own vision could not have been physical, it is clear that he did not think of the experience of the others as having been physical either; [9] nor of the future resurrection of Christian believers in any physical terms.

The apostle's insistence upon the absolute distinction between the 'natural body' and the 'spiritual body' confirms the point. The life after death is for him one lived not in these bodies which now we have, nor in bodies of this kind, but on a new plane and on wholly different terms. It is a life of the spirit: which is exactly the definition of immortality.

Let us remember that the Christians in Corinth, dull and petty and unscholarly as many of them seem to have been, nevertheless were Greek in their cultural tradition. Naturally, inevitably, they were disposed to reject what would seem to them the childishly material hope of the revitalizing of dead and decomposed flesh. St. Paul, in some ways fiercely loyal to the tradition he had learned in Palestine, and always eagerly concerned for the unity of the Christian fellowship, was trying to achieve a workable compromise. 'Look here,' he says in effect to his friends, these Corinthian Greeks, 'I know you believe in immortality and not in resurrection. I do too, for this is the only view that is intelligible. But for the sake of peace in the Church, for the sake of your brothers in Palestine who don't know as much as you do nor think as clearly: of course you can keep on believing in immortality; but won't you please agree to call it "Resurrection"?'

Thus, despite St. Paul's definition which transformed it into immortality, and which was designed to do just that, the word 'resurrection' maintained its place in Christian usage. That word inevitably carried with it its own original meaning, as well as St. Paul's transmuted one. (Shortly we shall need to notice another kind of transmutation involved in the apostle's thought; but that is on a level higher still, and we may have to wait to attain to it.) Through the years the intellectual confusion was further confounded, and even in our time we have inherited the confusion. Are we ready now to try to clarify?

What shall we think about life beyond death? In the first place, we do not believe in a physical resurrection, and really none of us ever did. We do not like these bodies of ours enough to want to carry them through eternity. Nor is it easy to work out the question as to which particular bits of organic matter ultimately should be assigned to which individual bodies. Aside from the continuing disintegration and replacement which inhere in the life process, the single datum of cannibalism absolutely refutes any notion that all human bodies can be raised again in their former constituencies of particular proteins. Logically, 'the resurrection of the body' is impossible. Morally, it is unimportant. We exclude it therefore from our further thinking.

In passing, however, we must note that we may not evade the issue of the 'resurrection' phrase in the Creed by saying, 'Well, I believe with St. Paul in a spiritual body; and it is that spiritual body which I mean when I say "I believe in . . . the Resurrection of the body."' We can mean that if we want to, and we may find it helpful for ourselves; but we may not pretend that the writers of the Creed meant that. The Greek and Latin texts of the Creed permit no such ambiguity as inheres in our com-

mon English version.[10] They read respectively *sarkos anastasin,
carnis resurrectionem:* and each of these means specifically
'resurrection of *flesh.*' Thus the early Christians tried to believe.
Thus we cannot believe.

The concept of the immortality of the human spirit, trans-
mitted from Plato through the later Greeks, is intellectually
much the more tenable idea. If there is to be any sort of personal
identity beyond death, it must be in spiritual rather than in
physical terms. If we are to believe in such continuing spiritual
identity, however, we must recognize it as being a matter of
faith and not one of knowledge. For individual continuity beyond the material realm there is no evidence so strong as to be
proof. Many of us would say that in the nature of the case there
can be no such evidence.

Moreover there are, as to the non-physical survival of
individuals, two major logical difficulties which we may not
ignore. One is the same question which arose when we thought
about personal consciousness as attributed to God. Can personal
consciousness operate without a nervous system? We know of
none that does. If we will, we may choose to believe that there
can be consciousness which is not physically conditioned. We
have neither empirical nor rational ground for arguing that there
is.

Still more weighty is the ultimate question of the reality of
time itself. To speak of personal survival 'after death' is to
assume that time is real, and that the time framework of our
present life inheres in the absolute nature of the universe. Yet
both modern physics and contemporary philosophy are driving
us to the judgment that time and space are not ultimate realities
at all: that time and space are merely categories which now we
use in trying to interpret our own limited experience. To reject
the concept of physical resurrection is quite frankly to set aside
personal survival in space. If time is not real either, time may not

be thought a condition of ultimate human value; and so the notion of life 'after death' loses all relevance to ultimate meanings.

Here the greatest of all the Greek Christians comes again to our rescue: to our intellectual rescue first, but gloriously to our moral rescue as well. The fourth Gospel rises above all quibbles of metaphysics in that definition of 'eternal life' which is this chapter's final text. The basic trouble with the historic thinking that we have reviewed, the trouble with our own questionings as well, is simply that attention has been centered on the issue of quantity. The vital question is not, 'If a man die, shall he live again?' The question that matters is, 'How shall a man live?'

'This,' says the fourth Gospel, 'this is life eternal: that they might know thee the only true God, and Jesus Christ whom thou hast sent.' Not quantity, but quality, is what counts: not how much of life, but life of what kind. Duration is beside the point. (Think of Methusaleh, of whom all that is told is that he lived 969 years, and then died.[11] Of what use, of what meaning, is Methusaleh's longevity to us?) Not the duration of life, but life's character, determines whether or not it is eternal. Eternal life is not that which endures forever in time. It is the life that is in harmony with those eternal truths which transcend time and space alike.

Specifically, for the Christian, eternal life is that kind of life which is found in the God who is eternal spirit and life, who is eternal light and love, who is eternal beauty, truth, and goodness. For the Christian, eternal life is that kind of life which is found in the living Christ. For the Christian, eternal life is that kind of life which we have called the abiding presence of the Holy Ghost. For the Christian, eternal life is that kind of life which we know in a holy Catholic Church that is truly a communion of saints. If this life in God and the Christ and the Holy

Ghost and the holy Catholic Church is our life, then we do live eternally: we live eternally here and now.

Thus, by recognizing the true nature of our problem, we are led inevitably: and triumphantly: from the physical and metaphysical realms into the moral. As to those who are gone from us, the very fact that we have been concerned about their destiny is witness to the eternality of their living. Had they not lived so as to make us care, their living would not have mattered to us then and could not matter now. Whether as individuals they are conscious today is a point for discussion; and the conclusion on that point finally has to be a conclusion of faith. That we are conscious of them is a continuing fact, and one which in itself gives life to us who remain. That we have loved, even though now we have lost, is for us enough. Those whom truly we have loved, we cannot lose. Those whom we have loved live ever, in the eternal quality of the life that was theirs: the life that therefore is theirs—and, through them, ours as well; and through us, the life of that innumerable company which yet shall strive to live.

Thus we learn that the question of the life everlasting is one which concerns not only our thought about the loved ones who physically have died; but also: and much more crucially: our facing of ourselves who physically are alive. To believe in the life eternal is not to accept an opinion about an unseen future. It is to declare a purpose and a procedure for the living present. The Greeks (and William Wordsworth with them [12]) were wrong on one point at least: that is, in their supposing that souls are immortal before birth as well as after death. Souls are not immortal, until and unless they become so. Life is not eternal, until and unless it is lived in eternal terms.

Here the concept of the resurrection may have moral meaning indeed, even though not physical. St. Paul's fondness for the term, despite his repudiation of its first and obvious definition, surely must arise from his intense awareness of his own personal resurrection from spiritual death. In this sense Christianity not only may, but also must, contend for the resurrection doctrine; but it will have to guard always against the dangers that belong to the common, fleshly history of the word.

How is a man's soul raised from the dead? How does his spirit become immortal? Quality, not quantity, must be the measure. Some have entered into eternal life at a point in time, in a great moral crisis which from that point on made their lives worth living. Some have grown into eternal life almost without knowing it, as their minds increasingly laid hold of meaning and as their hearts gained courage to deal with reality. The life everlasting for us is not in a future heaven. Eternal life is here; and for many of us eternal life becomes most real just when most honestly we face our present hell.

In so far as we know for ourselves this eternal life of quality, in so far as we live eternal life now, inevitably we shall transmit its quality to all whom we touch: the eternal quality of our life; or, if we should fail them and ourselves, we shall pass on the deathly quality of our life. We may not think to live only to ourselves. We may not think that our spiritual dying kills none but us.

If we do live now the eternal kind of life, we cannot be callous or careless about any human value, any human person. Those who died in the fighting matter: matter to us whether we knew them or not, matter to us whether they died fighting for us or against us. Those who live in this world's present madness matter too: matter still more, for there is more that we can do about their destiny. If we live now the eternal kind of life, we shall be neither morbid about the physically dead nor despairing about the spiritually sick. The dead are immortal in the eternality of their sacrifice. The living will become immortal as they find the eternal way of life: the living of whom we are.

'I believe in . . . the Life everlasting.' We can believe in it, for we have seen eternal life in hundreds of men and women we have known. We can live in the life eternal, in the now that is here and in the now that has no bounds of time. We shall live in the life eternal whenever, wherever, we have the courage fully and freely and faithfully to live. We do not know how long we shall live. We can determine how well.

17. I BELIEVE: THAT I MAY SEE

'Lord, I believe; help thou mine unbelief.'—St. Mark 9:24
(AV).
*'It is the spirit that quickeneth; the flesh profiteth nothing:
the words that I speak unto you, they are spirit, and
they are life.'*—St. John 6:63 (AV).
*'As no one can strive for that being, unless he believes in it;
so also to believe it aids no one, unless he strives for it.'*
—St. Anselm, about A.D. 1100.[1]
'I believe, that I may understand.'—St. Anselm.[2]

Shall we continue to say the Creed? I think we should; and I
think we should restore it where it has dropped out of use. But
there are two qualifications that must be stated: first, that saying the Creed is useful in direct measure as its essential meanings and values are understood, and no further; and second,
that the Creed is a means to the apprehension of values, to which
it stands as servant rather than as master.

The quick 'modernist' reply of course is that the values (if
any) are so far concealed by the Creed's words, are so hard to
get at within these forms, that this way of seeking for values is
not worth the effort involved. This answer rests upon the dual
assumption that the words as they stand are almost necessarily
meaningless or misleading, and that the gains which some of us
would seek by study and use of the Creed may be better secured otherwise and elsewhere. I dissent; and this is why:

Were the words meaningless or misleading in themselves,
they scarce would have survived the centuries as they have. To
declare that God and the Christ and the Holy Ghost, the Church
and the forgiveness of sins and the life eternal, have had and
have no significant content for men and women, is patent non-
sense. 'But,' says the objector, 'they have content only because
of the cultural setting, only because of the heritage of tradition.'
And so he falls into the trap.

It is precisely because of the cultural history which is ours in Christendom, it is precisely because we share in an infinitely rich heritage of tradition, that the Creed serves to bring together the meanings that are ours in the fellowship of the Christian faith. Its expressions are the symbols, one by one, of the best that we have known and the noblest that we can seek; and so its whole remains the Symbol of our united faith in total Christian value. The argument that we should drop it, because in our own shoddy and unreflective time its terms seem difficult, would apply equally to all Scripture, to Plato, to St. Thomas, to Schleiermacher—yea, and no less to John Dewey and Alfred North Whitehead. We do seek the spirit beyond the letter: but the letter is none the less the spirit's means of communication among men, and through men to men. We shall not know all the gifts of the spirit until we persuade the letter to yield to us its meaning.

That means hard work in any terms, for anyone, within any tradition of letters or art or religion. Are we so lazy, or so distrustful of our mental powers, that we must discard all those things that are 'hard to be understood'? [3] We have badly overdone, in American Christianity, our talk about the 'simplicity of the Gospel.' The Gospel is life, and is no more simple than life: life which can neither be understood nor lived without rugged effort of mind and will. Our life is a part of all history, and our Christian life is a part of all Christian experience from Nazareth even until now. It is a paramount obligation of the leader of Christian thought to know that history, and to make it known. It must be the opportunity of every layman, to the limit of his intellectual capacity (and lay capacity is less limited than some suppose), to share in that knowledge. To begin by throwing out the first summation of Christian faith is not to clarify, but to confuse and deprive.

Nor may we hope to solve the problem by substituting new words for old. Interpretation is needed, yes; as retranslation of the Scriptures is necessary in land after land and generation after generation. But the synthesis of experience and thought that be-longs to the Creed will not be achieved by one man, nor in a sin-gle century. The Bible is a collection of varied materials bearing upon the Hebrew-Christian tradition from innumerable direc-tions. The Creed is the distilled essence of that tradition, in its specifically Christian form, as seven centuries of intense living and thinking poured it into one vessel of a hundred words.

Shall we try to 'modernize,' without leaving something out? What phrasing then is recommended as substitute for 'God the Father Almighty'? How shall we state our judgment of Jesus, and our faith in the Christ, otherwise than in terms of 'Jesus Christ his only Son our Lord'? Is there in all our twentieth-century literalism a way of subsuming the impact of the man Jesus upon men more decisively and more nobly than in 'born of the Virgin Mary,' 'rose again from the dead'? Of course these are symbols: and all our terminology, including the words as words, is and has to be symbolic always. The choice is not be-tween symbol and reality. In the quest for the real the choice is between symbols that have endured, that have carried meaning for uncounted millions, and experimental symbols invented on the spur of the moment and untested by time.

'I believe in the Holy Ghost.' That is more readily susceptible of brief definition than are the Creed's phrases about the Christ: but what is gained by reciting instead, 'I believe in the divine presence in human life'? 'The Holy Catholic Church.' With that the Churches from time to time have tinkered, scarcely with benefit to themselves or to the universal fellowship of the Christ-ian faith. 'The Forgiveness of sins . . . The Life everlasting.' I take it that no Christian will profess that we sinners do not need forgiveness, that we ought not to seek the life eternal. Then why should we not join our Christian fathers in these declarations of the Christian quest?

The making of the declaration matters in itself, as an expres-sion of fellowship, as an urge to loyalty, as an impetus to life.

A Church service which includes no active, explicit proclaiming of common faith and common intent fails of one of the major purposes of common worship. We must pray, we should praise, we ought to think. But neither in prayer nor hymn nor sermon (though probably the hymn comes nearest) is the positive note of united conviction, the triumphant assurance of our united devotion to our chosen values. (And if really it is the symbolism that causes difficulty, what about the symbolism of Scripture and of hymns? To excise because we cannot take the phrasing literally would wipe out not only the Creed, but also the major part of the Bible and a good half of the Hymnal. Let the clergyman who rejects the use of the Creed but test his service materials for last Sunday.)

Positively, the Creed speaks both of faith and of life. To oppose theology to ethics, as the custom of some is, is to take from ethics its very groundwork and *raison d'être.* 'I believe in God.' That is an act of faith; but true faith in God drives to seeking the will of God, and naught but true faith can thus drive. 'I believe in Jesus Christ.' Jesus is the example, the Christ is the power: we need both in our living, and we shall not have them save as we begin by believing. 'Crucified, dead, and buried: He descended into hell.' Where in history have the claims of loyalty, the demands of human concern for humankind, the splendor of self-giving in humble service, been more mightily set forth? 'He shall come to judge the quick and the dead.' Some of us object to that, saying that we do not believe it. Don't we? Or are we just a bit unwilling to face his judgment?

The plea so often made today is that we should escape the bondage of tradition, that for symbol we should substitute literal sense. Certainly tradition has no right to hold us in bondage, and certainly symbolism must not become idolatry. But to reject tradition is to reject not only its possible binding, but also its positive and essential strength and light. To jettison symbol is to discard not only a potential idol, but also an actual beauty, and in all likelihood a precious meaning too. We cannot escape history, and we shall fare poorly without the symbols that history has given us. He who wishes may repudiate the Christian tradition, and its symbols with it; but let him be aware that in doing so he is letting go his grasp on Christianity itself.

In thoughtful heeding of the tradition, in creative using of the symbols, there is no repudiation of intelligence and knowledge. We shall not go all the way with Tertullian, in his 'It is certain because it is impossible.' [4] Tertullian wrote that after he had become openly a heretic; and it was that way that his Montanist heresy lay. The Christian faith does not contravene fact and reason, and in the hands of its truest and greatest interpreters it never has been held to do so. But the Christian faith does declare that fact and reason are not all. Did it not declare that, it would not be a faith. It is by the act of faith that the Christian begins to apprehend the truth; and it is through the symbols of the faith that Christians come together in their quest and in their finding.

'I believe, that I may understand.' None than St. Anselm had less patience with intellectual laziness. He demanded reasonableness, and vigorous reasoning. As later critics have pointed out, he no doubt claimed more for reason than reason rightly can supply. But he knew that the use of reason began to have significance only when the great hypothesis first had been declared and accepted. 'He that comes to God must believe that he is.' [5] And the long-ago Archbishop of Canterbury adds, 'To believe aids no one, unless he strives.'

These are the two essentials: faith and striving. The faith comes first; but its full fruition is known only in and by the struggle of life. We must strive to understand. We must strive equally to live. The Creed challenges our understanding. Once understood, and in so far as it is understood, it is available to strengthen mightily our living. Through the years the Church worked out its Symbol of the Christian faith. God is the beginning, the Christ is the center, and the end is the life eternal. This is faith, and this is life. In the Symbol then the meaning of the faith may be found: may be found by those who believe, who believe enough to strive.

NOTES

Chapter 1. I BELIEVE: I DO NOT SEE

[1] Rufinus, about A.D. 400, assigns the composition to the apostles as a group: *Exposition of the Symbol*, 2; *PL* 21:337. There are two slightly varying accounts of the distribution of phrases among the apostles in two sermons erroneously attributed to St. Augustine: Nos. 240, 241; *PL* 39:2189f. A third variant appears in the *Collection from the Several Canonical Books*, by the eighth-century Pirminius: *PL* 89:1034.

[2] This is another pseudo-Augustinian sermon, but the attribution to St. Caesarius is generally accepted. The Creed is stated in the imperative form, *Credite ergo, charissimi:* 'Believe then, beloved.' Sermon No. 244; *PL* 39:2195.

[3] I have not included in this list the *Quicunque vult*, the so-called 'Athanasian Creed,' because this formulation (which really is a canticle rather than a Creed) issued from no General Council, but was gradually adopted into Christian usage in the West. While its date is commonly placed in the sixth century, its authorship remains unknown.

[4] St. Thomas Aquinas, *Summa Theologica*, II, ii, Q. 1, Art. 5; Latin edition of the Dominican College of Ottawa (Ottawa, 1941), 3:1405a.

[5] Etienne Gilson, *Reason and Revelation in the Middle Ages* (New York, 1938), 83f.

Chapter 2. THE APOSTLES' CREED IN THE CHURCHES

[1] Tertullian, *On the Veiling of Virgins*, 1; *PL* 2:889.

[2] *The Teaching of the Twelve Apostles*, 7; edition of T. W. Crafer (London, 1920), 10f.

[3] Compare, for example, Acts 8:16, Romans 6:3, I Corinthians 1:13, Galatians 3:27.

[4] The use of the Trinitarian formula in the baptismal service is indicated also in St. Justin Martyr, *First Apology*, 61; *PG* 6:420.

[5] St. Ignatius, *To the Trallians*, 9; *PG* 5:681. See also *To the Smyrneans*, 1; *To the Ephesians*, 7; *To the Magnesians*, 11; *PG* 5:708, 649–652, 672.

[6] St. Justin Martyr, *First Apology*, 13; *PG* 6:345–348. See also 31, 46; and the *Dialogue with Trypho*, 85; *PG* 6:377, 397–400, 676.

[7] Arthur Cushman McGiffert, *The Apostles' Creed: Its Origin, Its Purpose, and Its Historical Interpretation* (New York, 1902), 48–57.

[8] St. Irenaeus, *Against Heresies*, 1:10; *PG* 7:549. See also 4:9 and 4:33; *PG* 7:997f, 1077.

[9] Tertullian, *On the Veiling of Virgins*, 1; *PL* 2:889.

[10] See, for example, Tertullian, *On the Prescription of Heretics*, 13, 36; *Against Praxeas*, 2; *PL* 2:26f, 49f, 156f.

[11] The text of the letter is supplied by St. Epiphanius, *Against Heresies*, 72:2f; *PG* 42:385–388.

[12] The entire text of Rufinus' *Exposition of the Symbol* appears in *PL* 21:335–386.

[13] The Latin text of the Creed of Rufinus, from which this is translated, is from his *Exposition* as cited in Note 12. That of the 'received' form is from Pirminius, *Collection from the Several Canonical Books*; *PL* 89:1034.

[14] Rufinus says that the clause 'he descended into hell' was in use at Aquileia, but that he knows it not to be included in the Symbol of the Church at Rome, nor in the usage of the Churches of the East; *Exposition of the Symbol*, 18; *PL* 21:356.

Chapter 3.   'GOD THE FATHER ALMIGHTY'

[1] (Pseudo-)Dionysius the Areopagite, *Letter* 1 (to Gaius); *PG* 3:1065. See also John Scotus Erigena's translation in *PL* 122:1177.

[2] William Saroyan, *The Human Comedy* (New York, 1943), p. 42.

[3] Isaiah 45:7 (AV): 'I form the light, and create darkness: I make peace, and create evil: I the Lord do all these things.'

[4] See John Scotus Erigena, *On the Divine Nature*, 3:5; *PL* 122: 634–637.

[5] St. Francis of Assisi, 'The Canticle of the Sun,' verses 2f, 9f; edition of J. J. von der Burg (Cologne, 1849), 151, 153.

[6] II Peter 1:4. Compare Hebrews 3:14, 6:4.

[7] Liturgy is necessarily a matter of symbol and poetry. It has been the effort to make liturgy didactic that has made it meaningless for so many moderns. God does not need our worship; but few of us will find God without the symbols and poetry in which we worship him.

Chapter 4. 'HIS ONLY SON OUR LORD'

[1] I have quoted here from the ARV because it follows the better Greek texts in omitting the phrase, 'the Son of the living God,' which AV includes from the Received Text. This addition, probably derived from St. Matthew 16:16, is of course a perfect example of the way in which the faith in Jesus, and its statement, were elaborated as time passed.

[2] The term 'rationalist' here is not used in the exact sense: I am referring to comparatively recent authors such as W. Benjamin Smith and Arthur Drews. The true 'rationalists' of the early nineteenth century stopped far short even of a partial theory of myth. See Chapter 9, notes 7 and 8, below.

[3] St. Clement of Alexandria, *Miscellanies*, 6:9; PG 9:292.

[4] St. Irenaeus, *Against Heresies*, 3:11; PG 7:881. See also St. Epiphanius, *Against Heresies*, 31:7; PG 41:488.

[5] In what probably is the earliest of his letters, the first to Thessalonica, St. Paul uses *Christos* alone (that is, without *Jesus*) once with the definite article, twice without it. In Philippians, possibly his last epistle, he uses *Christos* alone five times with the article, and twelve times without it.

[6] GH, *Again from the Dead,* a verse sermon for Easter Day 1943 (Eucalyptus Press, Mills College, 1943), [3].

Chapter 5. 'BORN OF THE VIRGIN MARY'

[1] St. Justin Martyr, *First Apology*, 21; PG 6:360.

[2] St. Matthew 1:18–25; St. Luke 1:34f.

[3] St. Matthew 1:16; St. Luke 3:23.

[4] Isaiah 7:14; St. Matthew 1:22f.

[5] Tatian's interwoven Gospel, called the *Diatessaron* ('Through the Four'), is the only early witness to the 'Joseph and his mother' reading. Eusebius charges that Tatian tampered with the Gospel text: *History of the Church*, 4:29; PG 20:400f. Theodoret of Cyrrhus declares specifically that Tatian excised 'all those passages that show the Lord to have been born of the seed of David according to the flesh': *Compendium of Heretical Fables*, 1:20; PG 83:372. This would seem to be a case in point.

[6] St. Justin Martyr, *First Apology*, 33; PG 6:380f.

[7] St. Ignatius, *To the Ephesians*, 7; PG 5:652.

[8] In St. Epiphanius, *Against Heresies*, 72:3; PG 42:385.

[9] Note the apparent change from *kai* or *et*, 'and,' to *ex*, 'from,' in Rufinus' version; see Chapter 2, note 12, above.

[10] While the dogma of the Immaculate Conception was not finally affirmed until 1854, it was urged as early as the twelfth century, and was very generally accepted by the fifteenth. A Feast of the Conception of Mary was celebrated in the East from the seventh century on, but without the attachment of the dogma in its later form.

[11] See Chapter 4, note 4, above.

[12] This too is the force of 'born of a woman' in Galatians 4:4; and here there is no sign of knowledge of the Virgin Birth tradition.

Chapter 6. THE SURPRISING SILENCE

[1] Quoted in St. Eusebius, *History of the Church*, 6:14; *PG* 20:552. The passage is unknown in St. Clement's extant writings, but there is no special reason to doubt its authenticity.

[2] See Chapter 2, above. Of the twenty-five 'Confessions' in Dr. Palmer's collection, none refers explicitly to Jesus as teacher, though in some of them there are brief references to his humanity and his leadership. The phrase which recurs the most frequently is the Johannine 'the way, the truth, and the life.'

[3] It will be remembered that it was the heretic Marcion who first suggested 'scriptural' status for St. Luke's Gospel, and thus paved the way for the establishment of the Canon of the New Testament. See St. Irenaeus, *Against Heresies*, 3:11; *PG* 7:884; and (pseudo-) Tertullian, *Five Books in Reply to Marcion*, 1:19f; *PL* 2:267-269.

[4] See, for example, St. Justin Martyr, *First Apology*, 67; *PG* 6:429.

[5] For the account of the bringing of the meteorite symbol of Cybele to Rome, in B.C. 204, see Livy, *From the Founding of the City*, 29:10-14; edition of William Weissenborn and Mauritius Müller (Leipzig, 1909), 3:317-323. Compare Vergil's introduction of Cybele ('Berecynthia') into the very beginning of Aeneas' adventure: *Aeneid* 9:77-92; *LCL* Vergil 2:116-118.

[6] See Lucius Apuleius, *Metamorphosis* ('The Golden Ass'), 11; *LCL* Apuleius 538-560.

[7] That the Church as a whole never accepted the wonder tales in the Apocryphal Gospels is a striking witness to the caution and conservatism of the central Christian tradition. Nothing does more to persuade one of the essential reasonableness of the canonical Gospels than does a reading of the tales that uncontrolled imagination created in the New Testament Apocrypha. For numerous examples see

Montague Rhodes James, *The Apocryphal New Testament* (Oxford, 1924), 38–89.

[8] I have not included the descent into hell in this list because I regard it as being primarily a statement of Jesus' human rather than of his divine nature. See Chapter 8.

[9] It is noteworthy that the fourth Gospel omits all mention both of the temptation in the wilderness and of the agony in Gethsemane. The point to recognize is that these human aspects 'had been made known in the Gospels' already in circulation when the fourth was written.

[10] Albert Schweitzer has forced a general reconsideration of the problem of Jesus' claims as to his own person; but whether or not Jesus conceived himself to be the Jewish Messiah, in no event can he be thought of as having used the Greek categories of the fourth Gospel.

Chapter 7. 'CRUCIFIED, DEAD, AND BURIED'

[1] St. Ignatius, *To the Trallians,* 9; *PG* 5:681.

[2] See Hebrews 9:22. It is not surprising, in view of the theological assumptions of the early seventeenth century, that AV should be cloudy in its rendering of this passage; but even in AV the reference obviously is to the law and not to the gospel; compare verse 23, 'better sacrifices than these.'

[3] St. Clement of Alexandria, *Miscellanies,* 6:9; *PG* 9:292.

[4] St. Clement, *The Tutor,* 1:2; *PG* 8:251.

[5] St. Clement, *Miscellanies,* 6:9; *PG* 9:292.

[6] 'Crucified' and 'was buried' were added at Constantinople in A.D. 381; but to this day the Nicene Creed contains no mention of Jesus' death as such.

[7] St. Ignatius, *To the Trallians,* 9; *PG* 5:681.

[8] Hebrews 2:18 (AV).

[9] In Richard Baxter's hymn, 'Lord, it belongs not to my care,' A.D. 1681:

> 'Christ leads me through no darker rooms
> Than he went through before,
> He that into God's kingdom comes
> Must enter by this door.'

[10] Galatians 2:20 (AV). St. Paul's Greek here is difficult indeed to render; and recent versions have found one way or another of dropping the 'nevertheless.'

Chapter 8. 'HE DESCENDED INTO HELL'

[1] Tertullian, *On the Soul*, 55; *PL* 2:742f.

[2] Rufinus, *Exposition of the Symbol*, 17; *PL* 21:355.

[3] See the same, 18; *PL* 21:356. Rufinus notes that the clause, though used at Aquileia, was not in the Creed as known at Rome, nor in the Churches of the East.

[4] The suggestion is that in the original, in Greek uncials, the text read ENOKAIENOCH, 'in which also Enoch'; and that a later scribe, thinking this simply an accidental repetition of letters, left out the ENOCH.

[5] I Enoch 13f; R. H. Charles, *The Book of Enoch* (London, 1921), 39–42.

[6] Ephesians 4:9f (ERV). I confess myself unimpressed by what seems to me the wish-thinking exegesis that would make this 'descent' refer either to the incarnation, or to the continuing presence of the living Christ. But even if one of these did represent the author's intent, the passage came commonly to be understood rather in terms of the 'descent into hell.'

[7] Acts 2:31 (AV). It should be noted that this is a reflection from Psalm 18:10, which the sermon has quoted just previously.

[8] St. Ignatius, *To the Magnesians*, 9; *PG* 5:669.

[9] St. Justin Martyr, *Dialogue with Trypho*, 72; *PG* 6:645. There is no reason to suppose that such a passage ever was included in the text of Jeremiah.

[10] This is unmistakable in St. Irenaeus, *Against Heresies*, 3:20, 4:22; *PG* 7:945, 1046. St. Justin uses in his supposed quotation 'The Lord God,' but St. Irenaeus has (in the Latin text which alone survives for this section) *Dominus sanctus*, 'the holy Lord.'

[11] 'Gospel of Peter,' 10:38–42; James, *The Apocryphal New Testament*, 92ff.

[12] Hermas, *Similitude* 9:16; *PG* 2:995. This is cited by St. Clement of Alexandria in his *Miscellanies*, 2:9; *PG* 8:980. St. Clement discusses Jesus' own preaching in Hades, at considerable length, in *Miscellanies*, 6:6; *PG* 9:265–276.

[13] 'Acts of Pilate,' Part II; James, *The Apocryphal New Testament*, 119–139. I have followed principally the account in that recension which James designates as 'Latin A.'

[14] This is peculiar to the shorter recension designated as 'Latin B'; James, 139.

[15] Apollinaris of course did not flourish until the fourth century; but the doctrine of the descent into hell came to be used against his teaching as it had been against that of the Gnostics. This was proper, in view of the fact that both the Gnostics and Apollinaris made essentially the same denial of the reality of the Lord's human nature.

[16] See I Corinthians 15:29. Surely the adoption of this practice by the Church of Jesus Christ of Latter-Day Saints was due not only to literal acceptance of this Pauline passage, but also and still more to the fact that the Mormons stood in the same psychological situation with the early Christians, believing in a single and newly revealed way of salvation, yet concerned for the saving of those loved ones who had had no chance to hear the new gospel.

Chapter 9.   'HE ROSE AGAIN'

[1] Arthur Hugh Clough, 'Easter Day: Naples, 1849'; *Poems of Arthur Hugh Clough* (London, 1898), 105.

[2] This section is absent from both the Sinaitic and the Vatican manuscripts. RSV rightly has dropped it into a small-type footnote.

[3] The shorter ending appears in four major manuscripts, of which the earliest is of the seventh century. Yet another variant is the inclusion of a considerable insertion between our verses 14f, in the fifth century 'Washington' codex of the Gospels.

[4] With the narrative in St. Luke belongs that of the Book of Acts, 1:1–12. On the whole this duplicates what appears in the third Gospel. A minor contradiction is the apparent reference to Olivet rather than Bethany as the place of the ascension. More striking is what seems to be a denial of the Galilean appearances reported in St. Matthew 28 and St. John 21, in the statement that Jesus 'commanded them that they should not depart from Jerusalem, but wait for the promise of the Father' (Acts 1:4).

[5] St. John 20:19, 26; St. Luke 24:31.

[6] St. Mark 16:5; St. Matthew 28:2–5; St. Luke 24:4; St. John 20:11f.

[7] See, for example, the works of Karl Friedrich Bahrdt, Karl Heinrich Venturini, and Heinrich Eberhard Paulus.

[8] The rationalists of course were highly naïve in their acceptance of the external elements in the Gospel stories. Assuming the substantial historicity of the events as recorded, they tried to explain the reported episodes in natural terms. David Friedrich Strauss demolished their position by pointing out that the question to be

answered is not, 'How are the events in this story to be explained?,' but rather, 'How did this story come to be told?'

[9] I Kings 18:17–23; II Kings 4:18–37; St. Mark 5:22–43 = St. Matthew 9:18–26 = St. Luke 8:41–56; St. Luke 7:11–16; Acts 9:36–43.

[10] It may be that this tendency was heightened, especially in the case of the fourth Gospel, by the Church's effort to counter the entirely non-physical interpretation of Jesus' whole life that was urged by the Gnostics. Compare H. D. A. Major, in *The Mission and Message of Jesus* (New York, 1938), 216: 'These materialistic narratives of the Resurrection are apologetic: they are not historic.' I am indebted also to Principal Major for calling my attention to Arthur Hugh Clough's poem quoted at the head of this chapter.

[11] 'The third day' appears from St. Paul on as part of the resurrection tradition, and no doubt is the basis for the fixing of Sunday as the day of Christian worship (at first in addition to, rather than instead of, the Jewish Sabbath). The gloss in St. Matthew 12:40, referring to 'three days and three nights,' which technically is at variance with the dominant Friday-to-Sunday tradition, seems to suggest that this detail also took some time to crystallize into a single, accepted form. The concept may have taken its origin in the common belief that the spirit lingered near the body for three days. Compare the account of the raising of Lazarus, where 'four days' (St. John 11:17, 39) seems to emphasize the miraculous character of the episode.

Chapter 10. 'HE ASCENDED INTO HEAVEN'

[1] 'Theophilus' may have been either an individual of this name, or the 'lover of God' in general.

[2] See St. John 20:17, Ephesians 4:8–10. These are at least as susceptible to spiritual as to physical interpretation, especially in view of the general tenor of the two books in which they occur.

[3] See Chapter 9, notes 2 and 3.

[4] The four Gospels exhibit much the same development with reference to the phenomena at Jesus' baptism as in the case of the person or persons whom the women saw at the tomb. (See Chapter 9, note 6.) Compare St. Mark 1:10f with St. Matthew 3:16f, St. Luke 3:21f, and St. John 1:32–34.

[5] See especially St. John 14:16–21, 25–28.

[6] Chapter 21 seems to be an anonymous addition, made at an

early date in the effort to authenticate the Gospel as having been written by St. John the son of Zebedee. Note St. John 21:24f.

[7] George Herbert Betts, *The Beliefs of Seven Hundred Ministers, and Their Meaning for Religious Education* (Cincinnati, 1929).

[8] Compare Tertullian, *On the Veiling of Virgins*, 1; PL 2:889.

[9] William Wordsworth, 'Ode: Intimations of Immortality from Recollections of Early Childhood,' about 1803, stanza V; Thomas Hutchinson, editor, *The Poetical Works of William Wordsworth* (London, 1906), 588.

[10] The original form of this prayer is from the Sarum (Salisbury) Breviary of the late eleventh century, where it is indicated for use at Vespers on Ascension Day.

Chapter 11.   'FROM THENCE HE SHALL COME'

[1] Northern Israel from the division of the kingdom in 933 B.C. to the Assyrian invasion of 722; Southern Judah from 933 to the Babylonian conquest in 597. To each of these may be added something less than a hundred years of independence (with some qualifications) of the united kingdom under Saul, David, and Solomon.

[2] Isaiah 45:1. Doubtless it was for doctrinal reasons that AV (followed by ERV and ARV) translated 'his anointed' rather than transliterating as 'his Messiah.' The Hebrew is unmistakable.

[3] See Zechariah 3 and 4.

[4] Daniel 7:13f.

[5] '*The* Son of man' in AV is tendentious; the Aramaic original has no definite article. JM renders 'in human form,' which indicates the real intent.

[6] See Daniel 7:1–7.

[7] St. Matthew 24:14. The mention of Daniel in the AV text of St. Mark 13:14, based upon the Received Text, lacks early authority, and no doubt is derived from St. Matthew. Nevertheless it is clear that the 'little apocalypse' of St. Mark is indeed dependent on Daniel: there are unmistakable references to Daniel 2:28, 9:17, 12:1, and 12:11.

[8] St. Mark 13:30 = St. Matthew 24:34 = St. Luke 21:32.

[9] After the Fourth Gospel, major contributions to the transmuting of the doctrine were made by the spiritualizing interpretations of St. Clement of Alexandria and Origen, and in the philosophy of history of St. Augustine. See especially St. Augustine, *On the City of*

God, 20:9; *PL* 41:672–675. Here the millennial reign is definitely said to have begun with the Christ's first coming.

[10] St. Matthew 24:23 = St. Mark 13:21. Compare St. Luke 17:23.

[11] II Corinthians 3:17. The text reads '*the* Spirit,' not 'spirit' in general.

[12] Galatians 2:20.

Chapter 12. 'TO JUDGE THE QUICK AND THE DEAD'

[1] Thomas à Kempis, *On the Imitation of Christ,* 1:2; edition of J. B. Weigl (Salzburg, 1837), 6.

[2] See also Chapter 6, note 10.

[3] 'Authenticity' is not to be confused with validity as to meaning. A statement may be authentic: that is, written or spoken by the person specified: without necessarily being true. To determine the matter of authenticity thus is not at all to settle the question of accuracy or of cogency.

[4] The evidence for the prevalence of such a view stands largely in the recurring prophetic attacks upon it; but in its own right it is apparent in many of the imprecatory Psalms.

[5] Amos 2:6 (AV).

[6] Isaiah 5:7 (AV).

[7] Zephaniah 3:3f (AV).

[8] I Enoch 38–69; R. H. Charles, *The Book of Enoch* (London, 1921), 56–90.

[9] St. Matthew 7:1f (AV).

[10] Thomas à Kempis, *On the Imitation of Christ,* 1:1; Weigl, 2.

[11] John Greenleaf Whittier, 'Our Master,' 1856. This stanza is the sixteenth of thirty-eight in the original poem.

Chapter 13. 'THE HOLY GHOST'

[1] It should be noted that I Corinthians 14, the *locus classicus* for New Testament discussion of the 'gift of tongues,' knows nothing of a gift of languages. The phenomenon clearly was the familiar glossolalia prevailing in some revivalist groups in our own time. The narrative in Acts 2, being without support and evidently unknown to St. Paul, cannot be considered factual.

[2] St. Mark 1:10 = St. Matthew 3:16 = St. Luke 3:22. See also St. John 1:33.

[3] Orally and informally at a meeting of the Pacific Coast Theological Group in San Francisco, in November of (I think) 1942. Professor Lanz was speaking of the monks of Mount Athos, whom he thought to know the Holy Ghost without having attempted to define.

[4] Thus ARV and RSV, throughout; though not ERV. (Perhaps I am just betraying a stubborn English streak in my own preference!) Notice also the most recent Methodist revision of the Creed: see Chapter 2.

[5] And the author of the fourth Gospel; see St. John 4:24, which should be read (as in RSV) 'God is spirit,' not 'God is a spirit.'

[6] American editions respectively 1923, 1922, and 1924.

[7] 'Jahveh' is the nearest possible transliteration of the divine name, commonly misrepresented as 'Jehovah,' which the primitive story-teller uses to identify his God.

[8] I follow the traditional dating of the early 'Jahvistic' narrative, 'J,' about 850 B.C.; but I would put the 'priestly' document, 'P,' nearer 350 than the conventional 450.

[9] St. John 4:24. See note 5 above.

[10] Read consecutively St. John 14:16–19, 26, 28. See also Chapters 11, 12.

[11] We scarcely would divide a Church upon the issue today. Nevertheless I suggest that the West had the right of the dispute: for has not the Holy Ghost come to us in special degree from the Son?

[12] As I type the final script I am reminded of George Santayana's account of the *Corpus Christi* festival in Avila, Spain; see his *Persons and Places: The Background of My Life* (New York, 1944), 100f.

Chapter 14. 'THE HOLY CATHOLIC CHURCH'

[1] St. Ignatius, *To the Smyrneans*, 8; PG 5:713.

[2] St. Irenaeus, *Against Heresies*, 3:34; PG 7:966.

[3] St. Cyprian, *Epistle* 62:4; PL 4:382. See also *Epistle* 71:1, 3; PL 4:422, 424; and *On the Unity of the Church*, 6, 14; PL 4:519, 526.

[4] *Synagogue*, 'bringing together,' was a comparable word in the Greek, and in St. James 2:2 seems to be used for the Christian assembly. Here the Vulgate renders by *conventus*, 'come together.'

[5] But not in the earlier American editions, nor in the British.

[6] Both in Greek and in Latin there is a verbal connection between 'holy Catholic Church' and 'communion of saints' which is not pos-

sible in English: thus *hagian ekklesian, koinonian hagion; sanctam ecclesiam, communionem sanctorum.*

[7] In an anonymous sermon previously attributed to St. Augustine, and probably dating from the sixth century: *Sermon* 240:1; *PL* 39: 2189.

[8] But the Vulgate has precisely *ecclesia* in this passage.

[9] See especially I Corinthians 12.

[10] Need a teacher footnote this? But I cannot resist remarking that the teachers are ranked third in a list of three.

[11] See I Timothy 3:1–13; 4:14; 5:17–20; Titus 1:5–9.

[12] In the third century the Old Testament 'priesthood' was carried over into Christian thought and organization. See especially Pope Calixtus I, *Epistle* 2:6; *PG* 10:126; and St. Cyprian, *Epistles* 54:5; 67:3; 68:8f; *PL* 3:502f, 995, 1032–1034.

[13] The narrative in Acts 6:1–6 presumably records the institution of the diaconate; and it is reasonable to suppose that something like this experience in the Church led to the selection of such officers.

[14] See note 1, above.

[15] St. Irenaeus, *Against Heresies*, 3:3; *PG* 7:849.

[16] Twenty-five years ago I picked up on Cornhill, in Boston, a sixteenth-century printing of Irenaeus; and found this passage annotated at great length in Latin, evidently by a monk who had thought the interpretation to be of major importance. His writing was so crabbed that, alas!, I could not tell what conclusion he had reached.

[17] But not the first evidence of Roman leadership; that goes back at least to the First Epistle of St. Clement, about A.D. 96, which clearly was written in response to a request from Corinth for Roman guidance.

Chapter 15. 'THE FORGIVENESS OF SINS'

[1] St. Augustine, *Tract IV on I St. John; PL* 35:2010.

[2] It should be remembered that Jonathan Edwards was no unlettered ranter, but an able theologian. We who may not find his sermons convincing nevertheless cannot deny their logical power within the framework of the assumptions of Edwards' time.

[3] Though I have referred to this as 'mythology,' I can cite authority for the tale. Elihu Grant of Haverford College, who lived next door to the Coolidges in Northampton, assured me that this indeed hap-

pened. (One notes that the Edwards tradition survives, in that Northampton yet hears sermons on sin.)

⁴ 'Joshua,' the Semitic form of the name, means 'Jahveh is salvation.'

⁵ St. John 7:53–8:11. The passage is lacking from the best manuscripts. One uncial places it after St. Luke 21:38, just before the priestly conspiracy against Jesus. In style and content the story seems better to fit in St. Luke's Gospel than in St. John's; but it is impossible to say whence originally it came.

⁶ I St. John 1:8 (AV).

⁷ I St. John 3:6 (AV).

⁸ Not so in the Greek, which would read *hamartolon,* 'of sinners,' as against *hamartion,* 'of sins.'

⁹ There is no Greek manuscript authority for this rendering, which belongs to 'The King's Book' of 1543; but surely what we should ask in prayer is forgiveness of our trespasses rather than of our debts. I suggest that a greater value than verbal conservatism has kept in use this form, as against the more accurate but possibly dangerous rendering in AV.

¹⁰ I St. John 2:3, 3:5f.

Chapter 16.   'THE LIFE EVERLASTING'

¹ Luis Monguió, 'Death and Poetry, Spain 1936–1939'; *Pacific* 2:3, 34–43.

² The phrasing of this familiar committal is based principally on the Sarum (Salisbury) Office of the eleventh century. It has undergone very little change in the successive Prayer Books since 1549.

³ Job 19:26 provides no refutation. The original text is hopelessly confused (as are most of the translations; compare, for example, the contradictory but equally inaccurate renderings of AV and ARV). Probably the best rendering is that suggested by Morris Jastrow, *The Book of Job* (Philadelphia, 1920), 264f.

⁴ Ecclesiastes 3:20 (AV). It is worth noting that even the pious interpolators who worked so hard on this book never thought to insert any reference to a personal future life.

⁵ Daniel 12:2f.

⁶ See especially Ecclesiasticus 44:1–15.

⁷ II Esdras (= IV Ezra in the Vulgate) 7:32 (EJG).

⁸ See especially Wisdom of Solomon 3:1–8.

⁹ See Chapter 9, pp. 77–79, above.

[10] See Chapter 2, pp. 16f, above.

[11] Genesis 5:21–27. Nor does Methusaleh appear again in the Scriptures, except in the Lucan genealogy, St. Luke 3:37.

[12] See Chapter 10, note 9.

Chapter 17.   I BELIEVE: THAT I MAY SEE

[1] St. Anselm, *Discourse on Faith Seeking Understanding,* 1; *PL* 158:227.

[2] *Meditation on the Essence of Divinity as an Example of the Intelligence of Faith,* 76; *PL* 158:220.

[3] II Peter 3:16. Words and symbols gave difficulty even at the outset; but the author of this little letter does not reject St. Paul because he finds it hard to understand him.

[4] Tertullian, *On the Flesh of Christ,* 5; *PL* 2:761.

[5] Hebrews 11:6 (GH). And the reward is still to them that diligently seek him.

INDEX OF BIBLICAL PASSAGES

INDEX OF NAMES AND SUBJECTS